The

4,000-Year-Old Reason

THEY HATE

Donald Trump

Babylon's Bid To Rule The World

Martinus Lucianus

Published by Dauphin Publications Inc. 2024
www.daupub.com

dauphin publications

CONTENTS

TITLE	page

Introduction: Our Present Danger

If you are reading this essay, you are one of the people who believe that the world, and especially the Western Nations, are in very serious trouble. You believe that we are on the brink of the worst financial collapse – perhaps – in the history of the world. You know this could result in a period of political instability as well. You believe that what used to be the bedrock for progress and stability in the world, Western Civilization, is crumbling and dismantling at an alarming rate. You believe that after World War 2, with the defeat of the Axis Powers, the darkness which came so very close to plunging the world into an incredible level of slavery and oppression, gave way to a euphoria which seemed like lighthearted freedom. This euphoria, has now given way to an apathy of the traditional vanguards for the foundations of culture and faith, and the repercussions of an entire generation who, in their newfound peace, had forgotten God, is devastating.

If you have been sent this essay, you are very concerned about the future. The dark forces of the world continue to align themselves against the net benefits of the structures which arose from the ashes of WW2, and seek to overthrow it. You see a world which has again become so vulnerable to collapsing under debt, corruption, and moral decline. You see powerful forces talking of a Great Reset; a making of the world according to what seems be the kind of world-wide control the Axis forces had in mind. You see them talking of the end of Democracy, Capitalism, and the Freedoms which are so necessary to their health—disregarding the incredible amount of good which the world has experienced as a result of their birth 500 years ago. You see a self-perpetuating-madness materializing within formerly "healthy democracies."

As a student of both History and Theology, what I present here is a succinct explanation of how all these concerns are interrelated and coordinated, stemming from some of the oldest forces that have been at work – quite literally, as you will see – since the birth of civilization. It is not hard to see what I am talking about. What I discuss and reveal in this paper was a reality of which many in the past were aware of, but were often unwilling to openly discuss. I am not discussing something novel. With a little digging, it can be uncovered and the pieces woven together. If, as we face the truth (which is the hard part), we are willing to look at anyone or any organization without rose-coloured glasses, willing to name names and connect dots, then what is happening to our world—especially to the so-called Western Nations—becomes clear. I'm using the case against Donald Trump as a prime example. He, as well as Western Nations, are facing a 4,000-year-old enemy, give or take a hundred years.

If we are willing to be ruthlessly honest, I suggest we will come to see very clearly that *the world is not falling apart, it is being taken apart.*

It is the foundations of successful economies, freedom, stable Western governments, and advancements in almost every area of life, which are hated. By whom? is the inevitable question. It is hard to believe that anyone would hate progress and stability, but I assure you, there are very powerful forces which want a return to the serfdom of the masses and Totalitarianism itself. Some of its collaborators are fooled into supporting them, some have been threatened into supporting them, and some of them are fully aware of what they are doing and are fully supportive of returning to the glory days of 500 years ago—when there was no such thing as freedom and progress... and absolute power dwelt only with the few. I know, because I have spoken to persons involved in this, and they have admitted as much.

They want the world taken apart so they can have *The Great Reset.* But what they want to "reset" to, is the way things used to be. It is not a new beginning, a *New World Order,* but a going back to before modern democratic republics, and Capitalism, and the freedoms which are now entrenched in much of the world. Since the end of WW2, it has been getting increasingly difficult to have a totalitarian government and business community—and, as far as they are concerned, it is this trend which must be undone.

I have written far more extensively about this in another document, but here I will try to explain briefly what we are facing. But before I go on, let me echo an article quoting "British writer, journalist and environmentalist Paul Kingsnorth, also a former atheist; My most strongly held belief is this: that our modern crisis is not economic, political, scientific or technological, and that 'no answers' will be found in those spheres. I believe that we are living through a deep spiritual crisis; perhaps even a spiritual war."[1]

Kingsnorth is sharing the sentiment of many others, around the world. What we will do here, is discover that he is absolutely correct. It is a war which has been going on for 4,000 years, and all indicators seem to be that it will climax before 2030. Let me explain.

---

[1] Trevor Tucker, *Western Report*, 21 Jan 2024

Chapter One
One Ring to Rule them All

Empires have come and gone over the last 4,000 years. There are books which record and analyze their rise and fall. What one will notice in reading these books is two patterns. The first one is that there is a similar pattern to their rise and to their falls. There is the building period, there is the maintenance period, and there is the decline period. Even within nations which have risen and fallen repeatedly, all that is happening is the same three steps are being repeated. This three-step pattern is also reflected in businesses, and they even have a phrase for it: *"From shirtsleeves to shirtsleeves in three generations."* Meaning, grandpa worked and sacrificed to build the business; having seen his father's struggles, his son maintained it; and the grandson, having (perhaps!) only heard about the struggles of his grandpa, ended up squandering it all. Nations are like that, too.

There is a second pattern which can be found in history, going back 4,000 years. It is the rise and fall of the primary nations at the center of the world, but then to notice how they are intentionally successive to one another.

The first stage is the rise of the first three primary nations of the ancient world. They are Babylon, Assyria, and Egypt. These made up the world powers of ancient history. Their centers shaped the culture and religion, as well as the political structures of the time. There are few exceptions to this rule. In fact, studies such as the one by Alexander Hislop, have shown that not only from these three cultural centers did all the religions of the Middle East find their origin, but even around the world there is evidence of their influence. Note, as just one example, the occurrence of Ziggurats (pyramid-type structures, but with flat tops) all over the world; in South and Central America all the way to China, Japan and in many other East Asian countries. These structures shared both a political and a religious significance which for us today shows the international and even intercontinental reach of their systems.

Then, in 605 B.C., a very famous and world-changing battle took place which changed everything, at least for the center of the world of the time. At a city in Assyria named Carchemish, these three nations met in battle: *The Battle of Carchemish*. Egypt went to rescue Assyria from the New Babylonian empire led by Nebuchadnezzar, and failed. Egypt fled for home. Soon afterward, the Babylonians came back and defeated Egypt so thoroughly that it never really recovered.

What all three of the former nations of (Old) Babylon, Assyria, and Egypt shared was a common religious ancestry and government system. They all went back to a great and significant historical figure named Nimrod (Gen. 10:8, 9), who was the founder of both Babylon and Assyria (Gen. 10:10, 11). Nimrod had an uncle, who was the founder of Egypt (called Mizraim at first, see Gen. 10:6, 13), and records show that these three cities were closely intertwined politically and religiously.

Nimrod had a son named Tammuz (mentioned in Ez. 8:14), by Semiramis (she was Nimrod's mother also, who was later given the title of "Queen of Heaven," as mentioned in Jer. 44:17, 18, 25). From them arose the religion of the Tower of Babel. So also did their political structure of totalitarianism. That, in fact, was the whole point of the Tower of Babel: to destroy individualism in the sense of freedom for self-rule and self-thought, with all being equal subjects of God's rule. Scripture tells us that the main reason God smote the people at the tower's construction site with a confusion of languages was that *all the people were as One.* The masses had fallen into a stupor of powerful groupthink united under the leading influences of their pagan leader, controlled towards one common goal: trying to exalt themselves to the very heavens with a central government out from under God's rule. To become like God by replacing him with their own rulers. To justify this type of government they developed the concept of a divinely appointed leader, who himself was in some sense "divine".

Before the Tower of Babel, the world was ruled in a republican style of government, or family government.[2] A republican government, according to Webster's dictionary means; 1. a government having a chief of state who is not a monarch..." and, 2. "a government in which supreme power resides in a body of citizens entitled to vote and is exercised by elected officers and representatives responsible to them and governing according to law." Think, for example, of the way people who went north of Assyria were governed (Slavs and Germanic), the concept of divinely appointed kings did not exist

---

[2] Rutherford, Samuel, *Lex, Rex: The Law and the King*; Canon Press, 2020 Rutherford, responding to the suggestion that Noah was the first king, and not Nimrod, writes, "No writer, Moses nor any other, can show us a king before Nimrod. So Eusebius, Paul Orosius, Jerome, Josephus say that he was the first king, and Tostaus Abulens, and our own Calvin, Luther, Musculus on the place, and Ainsworth make him the first king and the founder of Babylon. How Noah was a king, or there was any monarchical government in the world then, the Prelate [of the Pope] has alone dreamed it. There was but family-government before this." (p.84)

for them, even down to the time of the Romans and their conflict with the Germanic peoples. In the far East, countries like China and Japan had dynasties, but ruling families did not see themselves as divinely appointed, or see themselves as being "divine" in any sense. We would add to this that such republican-style governments supported independence of the religious leadership and political leadership. According to Pericles the ancient Greeks in Athens practiced a republican-style government, and was likely common among their cities,

Athens' constitution is called a democracy because it respects the interests not of the minority but of the whole people. When it is a question of settling private disputes, everyone is equal before the law; when it is a question of putting one person before another in positions of public responsibility, what counts is not membership of a particular class, but the actual ability which the man possesses. (Pericles, 431 BCE)

Put simply, it was Nimrod who began totalitarianism with the founding of Babylon, Assyria, and Egypt, in the form of individuals who ruled either by power or through self-appointed monarchies. Nimrod began the dual role of the Priest/King office. Power was concentrated into one leader. Some scholars consider Nimrod the founder of Absolute Monarchies, leaders who saw themselves as appointed to their position of Supreme Leader by the gods.

What the Tower movement did was exult the movement to centralize the power of both the political and religious power. It established what has long been the bane of freedom for the little guy; the autocratic rule of a small ruling class. When God destroyed the Tower and its system (found in Genesis 11), it was a declaration of war, for the position of Supreme Ruler had been that of God himself. The Tower's religion and government was a direct challenge to God's rule.

The three primary kingdoms in league with the Tower were Babylon, Assyria, and Egypt (Genesis 10:10, 11, 13, respectively). They dominated the world of many smaller kingdoms through vassal treaties, and sometimes fought with each other as well. The destruction of the Tower broke their unity, their alliance, their "one language." They were all Totalitarian, politically. Now they became Totalitarian independently. Though they still shared the same essential religion, their main deities were often given names unique to the three regions. Each of their religions knowingly had their origins in the religion of the Tower.

This was all to change when a powerful ruler revived Babylon. It was he (under God's direction) who overthrew the one-world order that these three kingdoms had exercised from the time of the Tower of Babel. By God's command, the world underwent a Great Reset, as Jeremiah explains;

Therefore the LORD Almighty says this: "Because you have not listened to my words, I will summon all the peoples of the north and my servant Nebuchadnezzar king of Babylon," declares the LORD, "and I will bring them against this land and its inhabitants and against all the surrounding nations. I will completely destroy them and make them an object of horror and scorn, and an everlasting ruin...." (Jer.25:8-9)

Nebuchadnezzar, king of the New Babylonian kingdom, won the Battle of Carchemish in 605 BC. This commenced a series of kingdoms who would rise and fall in succession to rule the entire region. It transformed the whole Middle Eastern world. The three old centers of power would never rise again to rule even the regions around them.

In fact, even Nebuchadnezzar's New Babylon would last just over 70 years, as under his grandson Belshazzar the nation was destroyed by an alliance between the Medes and the Persians.

But let us not get to this quite yet. First, let us briefly identify that there continued to be a competing struggle between the Totalitarian system of government and a republican-style of government under God, a struggle which had always existed.

Constitutional Republican-style governments continued to exist before and after The Battle of Carchemish. For our purposes it is important to note that Totalitarianism fought any government characterized as "a government in which supreme power resides in a body of citizens entitled to vote and is exercised by elected officers and representatives responsible to them and governing according to law" (a law not founded in a self-appointed monarch, but legislatively by its representatives). Even Israel, from the time of Moses to the rise of king Saul, functioned as a republican-style government which functioned not under the law of an earthly king, but under the law of God given through Moses; The Ten Commandments, and the book of Deuteronomy (this is why Samuel is told that it was God they were rejecting, not him; "it is not you they have rejected, but it is me they have rejected as their king." 1Sam.8:7, which God anticipated they would be tempted to do, Deut.17:14). The king of Israel, upon coming to his office, had to write out for himself a copy of Deuteronomy (Deut.17:18) to show him that he was not God, but God's appointee who himself was ruled by God's law like the rest of the nation. The law given to Moses was like the Constitution of the USA: it stayed in place no matter who the leader of the nation happens to be, and continued to be the law unto which both the leader and people were subject. It was a republican-style government and was an intentional rejection by God of autocratic man-led government. These were

Tower-style governments, like the one in Egypt, which God had rescued them from in 1446-1444 BC called The Exodus.

In addition to this, note that it is a great exception for a Totalitarian-style of leader not to claim that he/she is divinely appointed over the people. Not simply appointed, but literally acting on behalf of the divine. They believed their word is equivalent to divine, their authority is divine, and is above questioning by the common people. They *are* the law; a law to which they are not subject. Monarchs must despise republican governments, or their authority is threatened.

Finally, it is more than significant that it was the successive attacks of the three Tower of Babel nations which brought down and exiled the nation of Israel (Assyria in 722 BC, Egypt killed Josiah and exiled their king 605 BC, and Babylon completed the destruction under Nebuchadnezzar 587 BC). Because Israel had rejected their God, his law, and his government, He gave them over to the alternative: the rule of man.

To summarize, the government system of Totalitarianism, rather than being understood as the result of a person, was an idea, a concept of how the world and its people should be governed. This arose in direct opposition to the republican form of government which came before it, and which it continued to try and eliminate. Totalitarianism became "a ring" of power, a philosophical concept of authority which spanned individual nations and their leaders. Its principle was that people should be ruled—religiously and politically—by the few at the top. Those at the top are presented as separate and above the rest. And while they make the rules, the top is not subject to those rules. They claim, "not to be subject to the laws of men."

A perfect symbol depicting this is on the back of the US one dollar bill; a flat-topped Babylonian Ziggurat, where the top block is above (with the eye of the divine in it) but not touching the blocks below it.

Chapter Two

Four Successive Kingdoms Arise from the Ashes

The history of the nations which flourished because of the Tower of Babel had reached their climax by 605 BC. At the Battle of Carchemish, those three old nations were removed from influence on the world stage. Even Israel, by this point almost completely taken over by the religion which flowed out of the Tower of Babel,[3] was considered too rotten to be any good. God told the Prophet Daniel (chs. 7-12) that four "beasts" would come up from "the churning of the great sea" (7:3) and would successively remake the world's political scene.

When it says that they would come out of "the great sea", this is not hard to understand, for it means they would come from outside of Israel. Israel was known as the Promised Land, and the nations around her as the "Sea" whose waters would continually pound her shores (Ps. 69:1-4, 15, or, Is. 51:15,16). The four successive kingdoms of which Daniel was told, would come out of the nations outside of Israel; out of the sea.

What Daniel was shown (2:36-45) came along with the names of the first three kingdoms which God would use to remake the world; (New) Babylon, followed quickly by the Medo-Persian empire, and then by the Greeks, who would break into four kingdoms (8:19-25). History has shown Daniel's vision to be so accurate that some are tempted to proclaim that it must have been written after these kingdoms arose, and not during his own lifetime. They did arise, and fell, just as he was told they would.

By the end of these three successive kingdoms and their conquests, the former glory of the three Tower of Babylon kingdoms was rendered unable to rise again. However, their glory, memory, and religions were held in high regard by their conquerors, and in fact, their conquerors' religions were derived from the religion founded at the Tower. Alexander the Great, for example, died in the palace of Nebuchadnezzar in a stupor of drunkenness celebrating its former glory; an echo of the night Babylon's last king, Belshazzar died (Daniel 5:30).

What is key to understand is that the four successive kingdoms which overthrew the original three (Babylon, Assyria, and Egypt) sought power

---

[3] The "Queen of Heaven" reference in Jer.7:18; 44:17-25, and the men "bowing down to the sun in the east" (Ez.8:16), as well as the women of Judah "mourning for Tammuz" of Ez.8:14 are both references to the religion emanating from Nimrod and the Tower Religion, they being his wife & mother, Semiramis, and the child they bore.

for themselves by destroying the first three, but they did not seek to destroy their religions. Rather, they sought to preserve and restore them according to the understanding of their own interpretation (most of the gods which evolved among the Greeks have their roots in ancient Babylon). They celebrated both their political structure and their religious roots because all had the same roots in the Tower of Babel. They were all still Totalitarian, both politically and religiously.

Moving on to the fourth kingdom as revealed to Daniel, there can be no doubt about its identity. The unnamed kingdom can only be Rome. This is so for a few reasons; it is the kingdom which conquered the third kingdom of Greece. It acted just as Daniel had predicted. It is unnamed because at that time of Daniel's vision (circa 540 B.C.) the city of Rome was both too distant from Daniel's home for him to have known of it, and, it was too insignificant at the time to even imagine what it would one day become. It certainly fulfilled the predictions made about it in the Book of Daniel (crushing the kingdoms before it, 2:40; was plagued by internal conflict, 2:42, 43; and would exist when the God of Heaven set up his kingdom in the Messiah, 2:44, 45).

That the fourth kingdom was also the successor of the Babylonian religion is simply demonstrated.

First, Rome inherited Babylon's priests. The Babylonian kingdom fell under Belshazzar (grandson of Nebuchadnezzar). The priests of that city's religion were expelled by Darius in 331 BC. They fled to the king of Pergamos, an independent kingdom whose king welcomed them as representatives of the old Babylonians gods. Interestingly, the symbol the king of Pergamos adopted at the instigation of these priests was that of a "Divining-Serpent" on his headdress. This serpent symbol is the same as that used by Egypt's Pharaoh, and was ever-present in Babylon. This phrase, *Divining-Serpent*, in Latin, is *Vati-can*.

The presence of these Babylonian priests in *Pergamom* (old spelling) is referenced in Revelation 2:13, when it is said that this city was "where Satan has his throne." The kings of Pergamos began to see themselves from this time on as having a divine right to rule, a position bestowed on them by the Babylonian priests. When the last and final king of Pergamos, Attalus III, died in 133 AD, he willed by inheritance his kingdom to the Roman Empire. By this means the original concept of the divine right to Babylonian rule was abridged for a time. The abridgement would end when a leader within Rome took up the title *Pontifex Maximus*, and even the decorative ancient robes of the Babylonian priest/king office. That leader was Julius Caesar. The term's roots are from the ancient leaders of Babylon, and was used by other nations too whose religious/political systems were patterned after ancient Babylon.

7

Interestingly, when Julius Caesar crossed the Rubicon River, it was he who began a totalitarian monarchy over the Roman Republic as *Pontifex Maximus* in 63 BC. Note that Rome was a republic, ruled by the Senate, before this. Julius Caesar changed the government of Rome from a Republic to an Empire, with himself as supreme head of both the state and its religion; the very structure of the Old Babylonian system. Alexander Hislop explains;

When Julius Caesar, who had previously been elected Pontifex Maximus, became also, as Emperor, the supreme civil ruler of the Romans, then as head of the Roman state and head of the Roman religion, all the powers and functions of the true legitimate Babylonian Pontiff were supremely vested in him and he found himself in a position to assert these powers. Then he seems to have laid claim to the divine dignity of Attalus, as well as the kingdom that Attalus had bequeathed to the Romans, as centering in himself...[4]

Julius Caesar began to dress in the scarlet robes reminiscent of the old Babylonian kingdom, holding in his hand the rosier of Nimrod, wearing the mitre of Dagon and bearing the keys of Janus and Cybele. Clearly, he was inspired by the Babylonian priests. The first statue dedicated to the worship of the supreme head of the Roman Empire was erected within the borders, not of Rome, but of Pergamos.

Secondly, the Roman Empire also began to explicitly claim to be the resurrected ancient kingdom of Babylon. Many examples could be given to which even modern Roman scholars will admit; "The penetration of the religion of Babylon became so general and well-known that Rome was called the New Babylon."[5] Many of the statues of ancient Babylon were relocated to Rome for preservation and adoration.

Lastly, the title *Pontifex Maximus* was the ancient term for the supreme priest of ancient Roman religions (Rome was always pluralistic in its religion). But this term did not originate from them. Rather, it was adopted via the Etruscans, who were the spiritual instructors of the original Romans by their own *collegium*, or college of priesthood. The Etruscans themselves inherited the term *Pontifex Maximus* and their religion from ancient Babylon, long before Rome was of any significance. Therefore, when Attalus III of Pergamos died in 133 B.C., the title *Pontifex Maximus* passed on to the family of Caesar and resulted in both the religious and the political supremacy combined into one person. The ancient Babylonian religion, going back to the Tower of Babel, was given life again in Julius Caesar and his successive seven family members who would sit on the

---

[4] Alexander Hislop, *The Two Babylons*, pg. 190
[5] Faith of our fathers 1917 ed. Cardinal Gibbons, p. 106

Roman throne (this family line is likely to what Revelation 17:10, 11 refers).

But then the title was taken away from the Roman Emperors. The Bishop of Rome took the title *Pontifex Maximus* away from the Emperor of Rome, Gratian (367-383), convincing him that he was unworthy of it. But the title was soon adopted by the Bishop of Rome himself, in 378 A.D., a title he claims even to this day. By 395 A.D., the same pagan dresses Julius Caesar adopted from the old Babylonian priest-class, were now worn by the "Christian" priests of Rome; the dates and festivals of paganism were Christianised into church practice.

The term *Pontifex Maximus* means "Bridge Builder – greatest." This was thought of in terms of the bridge between the gods and men. This is how Julius Caesar conceived of himself, as embodying in himself while he held the offices of king and priest as the "supreme bridge-builder" for the nation. When Christians were confronted about their faith in Christ (who truly is the Supreme Bridge-Builder between God and man – John 1:51, "[Jesus] then added, 'I tell you the truth, you will see heaven open, and the angels of God ascending and descending on the Son of Man.'") the Roman authorities would simply state "Caesar is Lord." If the Christian did not say, "Amen", the truth of their identity was revealed. The Christian response was "No. Jesus is Lord." Meaning, the *real* Supreme Pontiff is Jesus, not the Roman Emperor—no matter what title the Babylonian priests had bestowed on him.

Other ways the term *Pontifex Maximus* was understood were as a bridge-builder between world religions, which is why Romanism was committed to pluralism and syncretism; the term "*pontis*" can also be understood as "absolute master" or even "one who can sacrifice" and "a member of a sacrificial college" from the Etruscans. In the Vulgate, the term *summus pontifex* was originally applied to the High Priest of Israel, as in the Book of Judith (Judith 15:19). In the Babylonian/Roman sense, the *Pontifex Maximus* was the head or "bridge" over an international super-pluralistic religion which thought it had a divine right to rule the world. What God had separated at the Tower of Babel, the *Pontifex Maximus* would seek to "bridge" back together.

What is clear is that the term *Pontifex Maximus* is not Christian at all. It has a long, successive history of political/religious leaders who saw themselves as having a divine right to rule, not only their own countries, but of the countries around them. The term is a loaded one, and the one who carried it saw himself as the Supreme Ruler of every nation.

It was in the midst of the height of this fourth kingdom that the most important event in the history of the world occurred. The prophet Daniel was shown by God that he would set up the kingdom of his Son (Daniel

2:44-45). (Quote) When Jesus refers to himself as the "Son of Man" in the Gospels, especially when the High Priest asks him to clearly identify himself "I adjure you by the living God, tell us if you are the Christ, the Son of God." (Matthew 26:63). Jesus replied, "You have said so. But I tell you, from now on you will see the Son of Man seated at the right hand of Power and coming on the clouds of heave." (V.64) This was unmistakably a reference to Daniel's prophesy that it would be during the fourth kingdom that God would set up his own kingdom (Daniel 7:13-14). At the height of Rome's power, Jesus was resurrected.

The kingdom of the Son of Man would not only be in opposition to the kingdom of Babylon's totalitarianism, but would be characterized by servant leadership. This is the very antithesis of totalitarian leadership. Jesus washes the disciple's feet (John 13) to demonstrate to them the kind of leadership his kingdom, God's kingdom, he was opposing Babylon's (see especially Luke 22:24-30). When Jesus sacrifices himself on the cross it is as a "Shepherd-King"; "The good shepherd lays down his life for the sheep." (John 10:11). In Totalitarianism, the sheep lay down their lives to preserve the King. The Resurrection proved that the republican leadership of Jesus had his approval.

In conclusion, the priests of ancient Babylon convinced Julius Caesar to transform the Republic of Rome into a Totalitarian system like that of ancient Babylon, with himself as supreme ruler over a Roman Empire. Rome took on the name *The New Babylon*, and the ancient Babylonian title *Pontifex Maximus*, the successor and preserver of the ancient Babylonian religion and political system. Thus, in Romanism, Babylon was alive once again. Further, like ancient Babylon, Rome incorporated into itself the title of both the supreme civil rulership and a supreme priesthood.[6] This authority, above and separate from the common people, civil and religious, was given to the Roman priests before the end of the 4th century AD.

The position of Emperor would eventually cease to exist over the Roman Empire. But the priest/king office of ancient Babylonian Totalitarianism would survive in the *Pontifex Maximus* of the Bishops of Rome, who often took the adjusted term of *Supreme Pontiff*. Later writers would begin to use the term "monarchial bishops" as a reflection of how the office of the Roman Bishop was being transformed into both a political and a religious office, just like in ancient Babylon.

---

[6] It is interesting to note that this blending of these two offices was the very thing which the Israelite king Uzziah attempted in 2 Chronicles 26, and for which he was judged most severely by God. This occurred in 752 B.C., merely two years before the city of Rome claims it was founded, in 750 B.C.—though in reality it was founded before this. One must wonder if in judging Uzziah, God was also judging an attempt by spiritual forces to overthrow the worship of God in the Temple. Those forces, having been judged, perhaps, fled to Rome.

Chapter Three

Up From the Ashes; Again

The Roman Empire continued to be totalitarian to the end, and though several attempts through this period were made to restore a republican style government, they were always unsuccessful. Once a leader has tasted the cup of supreme Pontifex, it is virtually impossible for them to be humbled into recognizing who the real Supreme Authority is and giving Him the glory (though Nebuchadnezzar did; See Daniel ch.3).

The Roman Empire suffered a series of military blows during the fifth century. Primarily these came at the hands of the Germanic republics to her north, and the Huns from the east. By 395 Rome had divided itself into two separate nations; the Western Empire ruled from Rome, and the Eastern Empire, ruled from Constantinople. The final and successful assault occurred in 476 A.D., when Rome's Legions in the Western Empire were so defeated by Germanic forces that most of them were never heard from again.

At the time, it seemed as though she had suffered a wound so fatal that Rome would never rise again. By that date, Rome as a political entity had lasted almost exactly a thousand years (509 B.C.–486 A.D.). When its tyranny over Western Europe ended, chaos ensued during Germanic occupation over such a large area.

Out of those ashes arose a leading figure. The Bishop of Rome became, for what was left of the western half of the empire, both its civil and religious leader. The title which had been reserved for the Roman Emperors; *Pontifex Maximus*, was now without rival in Western Europe.

From what developed, two dates are important for our purposes.

1. <u>600 AD</u>

It would take over 100 years, in 600 A.D., for the Bishop of Rome to take on the term "Universal Bishop" of the Church. This is the natural conclusion to one who claims to be the Pontifex Maximus. They bestowed that title on a man named Gregory the Great. He had rejected the title while he was alive, stating that, "If the Bishop of Rome ever claimed the title of Universal Bishop, he will have become the Anti-Christ." Never-the-less, after Gregory died, they declared him the first Universal Bishop anyway, against his wishes!

An "interesting" coincidence occurred after the Bishop of Rome took the title of Universal Bishop. Soon after he took on this title and presumed its authority, the Roman Bishop's efforts to exert this power over all Christians was renewed, including those in the Eastern Roman Empire which had not experienced what we know as "the fall of the Roman Empire." It was only the Western Empire which was destroyed by the Germanic peoples. They left the Eastern Empire to itself. For centuries before 600 AD the bishops in the Western Empire, which was centered in the City of Rome (the East's capitol was Constantinople), had the attitude of being first among equals. So often over the previous centuries the other bishops had to remind the bishop of Rome that the office of Bishop had no justification to Biblical authority over the others. Thus, when the Bishop of Rome officially declared himself the Universal Bishop, this automatically meant a betrayal to the other Christian Bishops (in Jerusalem, Alexandria, Constantinople, and Antioch). The declaration of the Roman bishop to be "Universal Bishop" meant that the others were called into submission. This claim quickly turned into Rome subverting them.

According to tradition, in 610 a visitation by the angel Gabriel informed Muhammad that he was the messenger of God (only 10 years after the assumption of the Bishop of Rome's authority). What we know for sure is that within the Eastern Roman Empire there were pockets of people loyal, not to their regional leaders, but to the Bishop of Rome. Because the Bishop of Rome wanted control of the city of Jerusalem very much, there is convincing evidence that he used influential Roman Catholics to prepare and shape the young Mohammed (Khadijah, Waraquah, the Roman Catholic king Negus of Abyssinia, and an unnamed Roman Catholic monk who not only introduced the young Mohammed to the writings of Augustine, but to the idea of the high place of adoration for Mary, the mother of Jesus, an adoration which continues to persist in Islamic assumptions about Christian theology). This resulted in the power and influence of all other bishops to be greatly reduced as Islam waged relentless war on them (and when they both grew tired, Rome attacked them both!) Unfortunately for Rome, and for the Christians and Jews living in the Eastern Empire, the success of Islam made the Arabic and now Muslim people unwilling to hand over Jerusalem as agreed when they succeeded in concurring the Eastern Roman Empire. This would result in many Crusades to "rescue" Jerusalem from the now "Infidels".

People who were not raised within Roman Catholicism cannot hardly believe that any organization could be so sneaky, so devious and duplicitous. But the evidence is not hard to find upon digging even just a little. Long before the revival of ancient Totalitarianism and the Roman Empire was realized in the Popish religion and government, the Bible told us of this enemy of God's duplicitous nature. When Revelation Chapter 13 says that the second "Beast" would arise out of the "land" (grounded roots) and not out of the "sea" (tossing to and fro) again, it means that it would arise out from the midst of the people of God. Meaning, the second empire of the "Beast" would arise from within the Church. The next line after this verse demonstrates this beast's nature; "He had two horns like a lamb, but he spoke like a dragon." That is, he spoke like he was a gentle, harmless lamb trying to serve and represent the Lord Jesus, when all-the-while there was another devious force lying beneath his words. He would be the most power-hungry person alive, and would wage war—just like the Roman Empire (the beast out of the sea)—on whoever stood in his way. Verse 15 says his goal is a spiritual deception; "Because of the signs he was given power to do on behalf of the first beast, he deceived the inhabitants of the earth." Always ask if you are one of those they have already deceived, because deception is his speciality.

2. 800 AD

In 800 A.D. Charlemagne founded what would become in Europe the Holy Roman Empire; the second beast of Revelation 13. Charlemagne would claim to rule by divine rite, an authority granted to him by the Pope. The Pope would wear a triple crown, symbolizing his claim to have authority in heaven, on earth, and in the underworld—as king of heaven, king on earth, and king of hell—where through absolutions, souls are admitted to heaven, while on earth he attempts to exercise political as well as spiritual power, and in his theory of "purgatory" he claims to have authority over souls after death. Among the words spoken when a pope is crowned are these; *"Take thou the tiara adorned with the triple crown, and know that thou art the father of princes and kings, and art the governor of the world."* This is the very position claimed by the ancient Babylonian rulers, the position the Roman Emperors had assumed.

It soon became clear that the establishment of the pope over Western Europe as supreme ruler could not be maintained without the establishment of authoritarian rulers under him, who were dependent upon the Vatican's support for the preservation of their own throne.

Therefore, monarchial thrones were established in England (Athelstan, 895-939), in France[7] (Charlemagne, 800), Spain (late 9th century), Germany (Louis II the German 843), Portugal (became an independent nation and

---

[7] The first king of what became the Franks was named Clovis I. His small kingdom grew through war, assassinating his rivals, and aligning with the Vatican after his Baptism in 496. It was Charlemagne's father, Pepin I who overthrew this kingdom in 741. Pepin was first anointed to this position by St. Boniface, and later, in 754, by Pope Stephen II. Further, according to Britannica, he had a strong desire to unite his empire with the papacy; "In 750 he sent two envoys to Pope Zacharias with a letter asking, "Is it wise to have kings who hold no power of control?" The pope answered, "It is better to have a king able to govern. By apostolic authority I bid that you be crowned King of the Franks."

took its own king in 1139), Denmark (Gorm the Old, ca.930), Norway (Olaf Tryggvason, 960), to name the major ones. All these rulers understood that their throne was largely the result of, and therefore they were dependent upon, the support of the Bishop of Rome for their position. Interestingly, Russia, with its own church bishopric separate from Rome, did not see an autocratic leader until Ivan's rule (1547-1584). Ivan carried on a correspondence with western European leaders. But even there, the Russian word *Tzar* and the German word *Keiser* both have their roots in the title of *Caesar* a title which he inherited from the Babylonian priests inhabiting Pergamos; where the Bible states is "where Satan has [had] his home." (Rev.2:13)

It would be a mistake to think that since the Bible mentions kings, the kings given their thrones in the Holy Roman Empire had some sort of Biblical justification. Rutherford demonstrates throughout his monumental book, *Lex, Rex* that the kings of Israel were intended to be shepherd-kings.

A king, as a king, and by virtue of his royal office, is the father of the kingdom, a tutor, a defender, protector, a shield, a leader, a shepherd, a husband, a patron, a watchman, a keeper of the people over which he is king, and so the office essentially includeth acts of fatherly affection, care, love and kindness, to those over whom he is set, so as he who is clothed with all these relations of love to the people, cannot exercise those official acts on a people against their will, and by mere violence.[8]

Meaning that, the position of king is nothing like the kings installed by the pope over Western Europe. Biblical kingship pointed kings to consider themselves as servants of the people, and not the people as their servants, "Slavery of servants to lords or masters, such as were of old amongst the Jews, is not natural, but against nature."[9] Western European kings, as Rutherford repeatedly demonstrates, were more like tyrants and autocrats, living in luxury at the people's expense and above the Law the people were subject to. Living, history proves, like little popes, like Roman Emperors, like the old Babylonian dictators.

Rutherford skillfully points out that even the kings of Israel were not "of royal birth" but were installed by the support of the people. The whole point of the royal line of Judah, according to Rutherford, was that it might set the stage for the Messiah to whom alone rightly came the office of king from birth, "It is proper only to Jesus Christ to be born a king." (p.121) When the Magi asked their question, "Where is he who has been *born* king of the Jews?" (Matthew 2:2), they were tacitly asserting the absolute supremacy of the child above all others. Harod, and every other king, was

---

[8] IBID, p.86
[9] IBID, p.94

not "born" a king. And after Christ's Resurrection to the right hand of the Father, he took with him that office, ending the Davidic royal line and making all kings after him without justification, but only challengers and attempted usurpers. Yet, kings were re-installed over Europe.

Soon after these kings were installed, pope Gregory VII (1073-1085) took "the right to levy taxes and hear final appeals from all individuals and nations concerning all matters, temporal and spiritual." He could do this due to his claim to be king of kings, for the kings he installed reigned under him and on his behalf. As one might expect, he assumed the role of the Roman Emperor, explicitly, "In addition, Gregory VII moved the pope's headquarters to the Roman Emperors' old Lateran Palace; having now claimed the powers of the old Roman emperors and having expanded these powers to cover the globe, he set up shop in the throne room of the old Roman emperors, where the pope's headquarters remains to this day. The pope then took the title *Augustus* from Julius Caesar, the first Roman Emperor to exploit this appellation fully.... The pope of Rome, said Edward Gibbons, is the ghost of Rome, sitting on the grave of Rome, and— one may rightly add—wielding the civil law of Rome."[10]

Under this authoritarian and totalitarian system of government Europe would be ruled (sometimes very tenuously) for a thousand years (800-1806 AD). In this was fulfilled what the Bible says in Revelation 17:18, a prophesy of the Woman on the Beast, "The woman you saw is the great City that rules over the kings of the earth."

These kings were unruly, often fighting with each other, and with the Pope. The position of supreme ruler is very corrupting, and tends to cause one to object to the rule of neighbouring kingdoms. And more often than not, the Vatican's Supreme Pontiff would incite them against each other so that none of them grew too much stronger than the others, and himself. Yet, most often, no king would have considered his crown secure until he had received the blessing of the Pope. They owed their right to rule as a divinely appointed ruler to the Vatican alone.[11] This, we shall see, is key to

---

[10] Brent Allen Winters, *Excellence of Common Law*, p.130. This book is rather expensive to purchase, but by all reviews, is more than worth the cost.

[11] It is often assumed that since Israel had kings, that the office of king should be accepted by Christians. This long-accepted assumption was shown by Rev. Samuel Rutherford in his incredibly influential book, *Lex, Rex: The Law and the King* to be absolutely false. In Question 6 Rutherford demonstrates, for example, that the kings of Israel ruled by consent of the people, and for the people. The kings of Europe were placed upon their thrones by the Vatican, and under Civil Law saw themselves as both above the law of the "civilians" and divinely appointed. Rutherford argues that the *Popish Prelate*, and the kings he established as his vassals, are contrary to God's will. Rutherford was condemned to be executed by the king of England for his book, but he was

understanding the era we live in, in the 21st century now that all these kingdoms are ruled not by those divinely appointed kings, but by a system much more difficult to control; Democracy, under a Constitutional Republic with Common Law, instead of Civil Law.

Internet websites are actively trying to whitewash this 1,000-year era as though it was not all that oppressive. Rome's involvement is being "massaged" as well. Hopefully they will not be successful. It truly *was* a brutal time to be alive. The subject's lives, be it in war or crusades or in abject poverty, were at the disposal of the monarch and the Pope, to aid them in the maintenance of their supreme power. They were the king's "subjects," alive to serve him. Those who came out of this era in the 16th century did not brand it the "Middle Ages" as though it were simply in the middle of two ages. They saw it as "The Dark Ages", due to the incredible oppression of those who lived within either the Eastern or Western half of where the Roman Empire used to be.

---

disappointed to have to report that he, "had been summoned to a higher king than he" as he was on his deathbed and soon have to depart. He would have preferred to meet the King of kings, having been martyred for his kingdom.

Chapter Four

God Raises up a Dissenting Voice

If a study of the history of political structures could be grouped into two broad groups, those two groups would be that of Totalitarianism and Republicanism. One suppresses freedom of enterprise, speech, thought, and of self-rule. It consolidates power into the few, who are above the law. Consolidation is the mark of the various forms Totalitarianism would take throughout history. The law is called the *Civil Law*, because it is a law for the civilians. It does not apply to the king, the pope or his priests. The other encourages just the opposite; and the law is called "Common Law" because it is common to all, including even the king. A study of the years 800-1806 AD reveals that oppression of personal freedom was suppressed all around the world. It was the Golden Era of government and religious domination by the few over the many.[12] There were very few exceptions, if any. Be glad you are alive now, and not alive then.

Rome was only different in one way from the rest of the other empires; It intentionally saw itself as the preserver of the Totalitarian legacy from ancient Babylon. It saw itself, therefore, as having a divine right over all governments and all religions, especially as it was during in its second 1,000-year-reign. Through that millennium it gradually built-up a system of laws and doctrines in which it saw itself as more supreme than any government which had ever existed, and rather as the one to whom all of them are accountable.

However, during this time, while Roman oppression was at its very height of power, God signified that freedom had not been defeated. The Bible, which Rome in both its 1,000-year empires had oppressed and persecuted, was finally, gradually, and with much resistance, set free. Few people in the year 1500 A.D. could read, including Roman Catholic priests. And if they could, the Bible was only available in Latin (the Greek and Hebrew copies were kept hidden from the public), which only a few select people could read. Some, against Rome's wishes, had translated the Bible into a language the people could understand (John Wycliffe and William Tyndale are early examples, but there were others in the late 15th and early

---

[12] I spoke to a Jewish Rabbi about this time period being oppressive. His reply was that the 200 years, between 1300-1500, are considered by them to be their Golden Era. Islam also considers this era a highpoint in their successfulness. Roman Catholicism also considers this a Golden Age for their power. It was the Reformation rising in the early 1500s which slowly dismantled these The Dark Ages.

16th century). For those who defied the pope's edict, life was cruel. The Bible is that power which frees the minds of men from oppression. It was, therefore, very forbidden, and even illegal to read. Often, those found with one were burned with it.

What one does notice though, is that in response to the Protestant Reformation the monarchies all over Europe during the 16th and 17th centuries began claiming for themselves a stronger form of *absolute power*.[13] They were now not only above the law; they *were* the law and not subject to anyone nor any law. They claimed to have received their power from God, through the pope, and were not among the common people. In England the debate was summarized this way, in Latin, is it *Lex Rex* or *Rex Lex*? Is the law king, or is the king law. Are leaders appointed by God, through the Pope, and are therefore not subject to the laws they make for the people to be governed by? This was the form of government which Egypt had, and Assyria, and Babylon.[14] It is the conflict of the two ancient government systems going all the way back to the Tower of Babel; totalitarianism and republicanism.

The struggle, according to a *Washington Post* article by David Kopel, was taken up in 1644, when the Scottish Presbyterian Samuel Rutherford published "Lex, Rex, or the Law and the Prince." The point of the title was

---

[13] The rise of Cardinal Richelieu 1585-1642) was not only brutal to those who believed the Bible, but was a powerful effort to restore the power of the monarchy in France which was weakened by the protestant Huguenots (who sought a more republican-style government). The murder of the Huguenots is what eventually resulted in the cruel oppression of the monarchy, the rich and the priests, over the French populous. This eventually ended in their going to the guillotine in the French Revolution. In the end, France became a Republic and abolished both the priests and the monarchy.

[14] If one is looking for a symbol of this form government, one only needs to look on the back of a US one dollar bill. It is called *the unfinished pyramid*, one block out of thirteen, above yet separate from the rest. But the symbol has a much older history than the US. The eye has its roots in *The Eye of Horus* and *The Eye of Ra*, two prominent gods of Egypt. The roots these two Egyptian entities are in even older Babylonian gods. That the symbol made its way into the Vatican, see the painting *Supper at Emmaus* by the Italian painter Jacopo Pontormo, as well as in many pieces of art in Roman churches. It is the symbol of totalitarianism; the one-thirteenth who rule over and separate from the common body of people in the place of God (thus, the all-seeing-eye placed in the center of it), just like the government of ancient Egypt. It is a little bit unnerving that at the Last Supper the thirteenth person who was at the table, left part-way through. Thinking that he knew better than everyone else at the table what should be done; he handed Jesus over to the Jewish rulers.

that the law precedes the king; the monarch must obey the law. "Lex, Rex" refuted the royal absolutists who claimed *rex est lex loquens* — the king is the law speaking.

The antecedent for King Charles's principle was the despotism of the late Roman Empire. The antecedent for Rutherford's was the Old Testament. There, the definition of the Hebrew nation is the people who live according to the law given by God. The Anglo-American ideal of "the rule of law" embodies Rutherford's principle. The law, not the individual who heads the government, is the supreme ruler. The true source of law is not the king's will, but God's will. King-made "law" that is inconsistent with God's law of natural justice and goodness is mere pretend law, not true law.

In the early 1500s the Protestant Reformation took Europe by storm. It challenged the political, monarchial, and religious monopolies which ruled Europe. The Bible was set free. This brought both religious *and* civil freedoms, which in turn undermined their absolute rule. In the very areas where Totalitarianism claimed supreme authority, the Bible taught belonged to God alone. Only God is Lord of Heaven, Earth, and under the Earth (through his Christ).[15] And politically, no man has the divine right to rule over others. All humans are subject to the Law, and are to be treated equal under the Law. For while all are made in the image of God, none, including kings and popes, are God implicitly. Only God is above the Law, which emanates from his character; the very thing these kings claimed for themselves.

Now, I do not know, reader, if you believe the Bible or not. But what you must understand is that it was exposure to the Bible and what it taught which caused Western republican-democracy and economic systems (Capitalism) to be formed. This is the root of the inherent freedoms which are so important to the formation of Western Civilization.

Some claim that it was the Renaissance which built the modern world, but this is simply not true. The Renaissance could not resist Rome's armies, Rome's armies did not fight against it (which is telling). Rome formulated a huge doctrinal statement condemning, point by point, anyone who believed any one of the doctrines of the Protestants understanding of the Bible; The Canons of Trent. It was the Protestant Reformation with its power to transform the human mind by the Spirit of God toward innovation and healthy morality. It was the Protestant Reformation and its doctrine that

---

[15] See Philippians 2:9-11; "Therefore God exalted Him to the highest place and gave Him the name above all names, that at the name of Jesus every knee should bow, in heaven and on earth and under the earth, and every tongue confess that Jesus Christ is Lord, to the glory of God the Father."

faith in Jesus as the one through whom, by his suffering and death, and Resurrection, a person can be put in a right relationship with God—which miraculously changes the heart and mind of the believer—which was the victory over Totalitarianism. This created an atmosphere for what would rebuild Europe, and from there the world, to flourish. There are many books which demonstrate this fact.[16] One of them was written recently by a scholar, speaker and writer from India, urging western nations not to forget their roots, for their own sakes, as well as for the sake of the rest of the world.[17] In addition, there is a video on YouTube of an Arabic scholar being interviewed on a Saudi TV station which is important to see. There, in the Islamic heartland one can see this honest man passionately defend the reality of the truth of what I am saying here; that it is the West, almost completely alone, which has produced *all* the progress and success our modern world presently experiences.[18]

When we see The Industrial Revolution, the stamping out of Piracy around the world, an end to slavery (which had been practiced around the world for thousands of years, by and of all cultures)[19], advances in the sciences, rights for women, and so much more, we need to point out, all found their inspiration within the rise of nations rooted in the Protestant Reformation. The nations which either openly or subversively opposed them were from nations and movements which were Totalitarian in their politics or religion (especially those which were ruled from Rome). In fact, the monarchies of the world (who were allied with the super-rich) worked together to resist the rise of republican style governments and their

---

[16] The list could be extensive, but a sampling is; *The Protestant Ethic and the Spirit of Capitalism*, By Max Weber; *How the Scots Invented the Modern World: The True Story of How Western Europe's Poorest Nation Created Our World & Everything in It*, by Arthur Herman; *How the Scots Invented Canada*, by Ken McGoogan. One asks, what made the Scots such a powerhouse? The only answer is *Presbyterianism*, which arose out of the Protestant Reformation. See also, *A Life of John Calvin: A Study in the Shaping of Western Culture*, by Alister E. McGrath.

[17] *The Book that Made Your World: How the Bible Created the Soul of Western Civilization*, by Vishal Mangalwadi.

[18] This video has been cut at many parts, not for length, but because of the biting evidence this man brings forward. But even what remains should make clear that it was the West which built the world, and the Bible which built the West: *A Wise Honest Arab Muslim Man Tells Muslims The Truth About Themselves*; https://www.youtube.com/watch?v=hZZMXV_PRXk.

[19] The word "slavery" comes from the word "Slav" or the Slavic people, showing how prominent white slaves had been in history. Note that it was the British and American nations which stamped out international slavery—the two most predominantly Christian nations of the time—at great cost to themselves.

constitutions.

As early as the beginnings of the Reformation itself, many Protestant writers and thinkers were identifying the inherent threat of Reformation to the power of the Papacy, and the totalitarian state it sought to impose on all the kingdoms under its influence. John Donne, metaphysical poet and writer, penned in *Ignatius and His Conclave* a telling satire that pits Ignatius in hell, trying win himself a higher seat of power in that realm. Through this satirical discourse between Ignatius and Lucifer, the reader sees an open criticism indicative of what new Protestants were seeing in the Catholic Church's reaction to the broadening freedoms of thought and governance brought about by reformation. Igantius tells Lucifer of how "the minds of Lucifer, the Pope, and Ignatius, (persons truly equivocal) have raised to life againe the language of the Tower of Babel, so long concealed, and brought us againe from understanding one another". The same patterns of the religion of Babylon, and the Tower of Babel itself, were springing up once more in the Church of Rome, and this was a basic imperative behind the motivations of the Reformers to establish alternate forms of governance and economy outside of Papal scope.[20]

The Revolutions all over Europe beginning in the late 1700s were different than previous ones, which were often one totalitarian rule seeking to replace another totalitarian rule; be it a military dictator or monarchial. The rise of Protestantism sparked Revolutions against tyranny all together, and had as their goal the freedoms now found in the West.

Think of the Revolutions of that era; were they not the overthrow of their supposedly "divinely appointed" totalitarian leaders? The overthrow movement was given life as the Protestant movement spread.[21] When the American Revolution of (1775-83) took a hold among the Americans, who were almost all Protestants, rejecting the British monarchy's rule, these movements then began elsewhere in earnest. A second revolution occurred in America when their form of government was changed from a federalist

---

[20] *The Complete Poetry and Selected Prose of John Donne*, by The Modern Library, 1952.

[21] The Glorious Revolution, also called "The Revolution of 1688" and "The Bloodless Revolution," took place from 1688 to 1689 in England, and was before the American Revolution. It involved the overthrow of the Catholic King James II, who was replaced by his Protestant daughter Mary and her Dutch husband, William of Orange. Interestingly, it was the Catholic King James who sought to move the crown to an absolute monarchy, while Mary and William abided by their Protestant convictions and strengthened the power of Parliament. The crown was reduced to a constitutional monarchy.

to a republican structure, with the election of Thomas Jefferson (1800).[22]

Then came the monarchical disruptions of the French Revolution and the Vatican (1789)[23]; the Haitian Revolution against the French Monarchy (1791)[24]; slave revolts occurred throughout the chain of islands between Florida and South America (1750-1800); the Greeks also threw off the tyrannical Ottomans (1821); the Balkan Revolution, also from the Ottomans (1804-17); the Mexican and Bolivar Revolutions which overthrew the rule of the Spanish Monarchy (1810-24)[25]; the Polish people sought to overthrow the Monarchies which traded their land back and forth as if it belonged to them (1830s); the Indian Revolution from the British Monarchy (1853); the German Reich, beginning in the early 1800s to 1872 continually tried to limit and restrict the powerful influence of Vatican control in its lands; and finally, the Italian overthrow of the Papal State's monarchy, transforming Italy into its own nation (1870). England was often close to having its own Revolution during this period, but its 600-year history of resisting Totalitarianism (and with the influence of Protestantism) led towards less violent political routes.[26] The Russian Revolution over the

---

[22] Few realize that this change was so dramatic. For example, when the Federalists controlled the Presidency and the Congress, laws were passed which strengthened the power of the few at the top; the Federalists. Visitors to the White House were to bow when greeting the President. When Jackson was elected, visitors were strongly encouraged to shake hands with the President, erasing the memory of bowing like a subject, as was done in Europe. The Federalists feared for their lives; the guillotines in France could be set up on Capitol Hill, too.

[23] Napoleon made the fatal mistake of proclaiming himself Emperor in the hopes of a stable monarchy. This, the French would not tolerate, for it was a return to a dictatorial government. Sales of church land were confirmed, and rural France emerged as a nation of strongly independent peasant proprietors. Sadly, the French returned to being ruled by the Papal monarchy, and it was only after WW2 they rejected it. They made the connection between the Nazis dictators and the Vatican.

[24] Sadly, the Papal monarchy replaced the French one.

[25] Sadly, the Papal monarchy replaced the Spanish one.

[26] The island now known as the United Kingdom has long resisted "divine rule" through an earthly representative, whatever form it might take. In the 13th century a British Parliament was formed, which produced the Magna Carta— giving the English people a voice to counter the king. This led to another revolt in 1341, resulting in a meeting house being established where the common people met separately from the monarchy, an alternative voice to king and parliament—which became known as The House of Commons. When king Charles I claimed the right to Divine Rule (a concept inherited via the Vatican

dictatorship of the Tzar was late in coming and, without influence from Protestantism and with the heavy influence of Roman priests over the main actors,[27] simply brought about yet another form of totalitarian government: Communism (1917). [28]

John Cornwell has extensively studied this time period, and summarizes;

---

and its claim of Apostolic authority), he was executed, and the concept of the separation of Crown and State/King and Country was established in 1689. The battle in Great Britain to be rid of the Pope's concept of the Divine Right to rule was accomplished by the defeat of King James II. James, the last Roman Catholic monarch over England, Scotland, and Ireland, attempted to reassert the right to unaccountable power in the crown by using military force. However, the Parliament had one last hope of resisting Totalitarianism in not only James, but in his greatest supporter, the Pope. Parliament appealed to the Dutchman, William of Orange and his English royal queen, Mary, for rescue. William invaded with a large force, and after defeating James II (who were aided by French Roman Catholic forces), were crowned King and Queen of England by the Parliament. This produced in Great Britain, The Bill of Rights, which greatly strengthened the rights of the common people.

But what ultimately saved England from its own Revolution of Revolutionary period of the 18th century was The Great Awakening revival of Christianity (which began with a Prayer Meeting on 1 January, 1739), led by George Whitfield in both England and America. This was helped along by the political efforts of John Wilke, The Hero of Liberty, who championed "the reduction of concentrated Power, and the right of printers to publish the debates in Parliament unedited." Wilkes spent most of his life highlighting the inherent dangers of Centralization and defending the necessity of the Decentralization of political powers. His efforts to oppose a system in Britain where the few control the many – essential to all forms of totalitarianism – and to show the wisdom of representative government were monumental. Thus, Britain was saved from Revolution by a rise in Protestantism and by those like Wilkes who applied the form of Government naturally arising from it.

[27] The influence of the Vatican in the Russian Revolution was shadowy. The Jesuit influence in and over the lives of Leon Trotsky, Vladimir Lenin, Carl Marx, Joseph Stalin, as well as in the life of Adolf Hitler (whose *Mein Kampf*, there is little doubt, was written by a Jesuit ghost writer from Farm Street in London). And 1917 Tsarist bank notes can be found with the hidden swastika symbol on display behind the Russian imperial eagle.

[28] After the Revolution, the Bolsheviks betrayed the Jesuits, keeping the Tzar's wealth for themselves. This is likely the reason for the Pope's vitriolic condemnation of Russian Communism, and of Hitler's foolish invasion of Stalin's Russia.

"Most of the modernizing states of Europe were inclined to separate Church from State (or, in the more complex reality of oppositions, throne from altar, papacy from empire, clergy from laity, sacred from secular). The Catholic Church became an object of oppression in Europe through much of the nineteenth century; its property and wealth systematically plundered; religious orders and clergy depraved of their scope for action; schools taken over by the state or shut down. The papacy itself was repeatedly humiliated (Pius VII and Pius VIII were held prisoner by Napoleon), and the papal territories had been in constant danger of dismemberment and annexation as the forces for Italian unity and modernization gathered strength."[29]

A critical year was seen in 1870, for it was this year in which the Vatican lost its right to a Papal monarchy over its Italian states. It was also this year (December 8, 1869 - October 20, 1870) in which the Vatican held the First Vatican Council. It was this year that the Vatican voted to greatly extend the powers of the office of the Pope—rather than humble them— declaring that he could speak *Ex Cathedra*, the very words of God with the authority of God, and that any Roman Catholic who disagreed would be excommunicated. This ended discussion and disagreement among their religious leadership, at least officially. This was a level of authority which no person in history had ever claimed, even Nimrod himself. This was Rome's response to their loss of power over Europe.

The countries which remained loyal to the Vatican, and still maintained their own monarchies, were strengthened. For example, in 1876 a new constitution established Spain as a constitutional monarchy, granting the monarch immense powers. Despite the trend to end totalitarian governments throughout Europe, and much of the Western world, Roman Catholicism was going in the opposite direction. Republican-democratic governments were on the rise, and the Vatican had to play her cards very carefully. She had to make an appearance of being cooperative. Then, in 1903, the Vatican declared that it had changed its mind toward democracy; it was now considered a legitimate form of government (but unofficially, it continued to condemn its principles). Before this, it considered the right to choose one's own government leaders, *illegal*.

This is the spirit of the Tower of Babylon, which long ago came to reside in Rome. It inspired Julius Caesar to change Rome from a constitutional republic to an empire, and that spirit continued down through the centuries. It is the spirit behind what caused the murder of 50-70,000 Huguenots (French Protestants) on a weekend in 24 August, 1572. When the Vatican heard of the murders, he threw a huge party, and struck a coin in celebration of the victory over these God-loving and Bible believing

---

[29] *Hitler's Pope: The Secret History of Pius XII*, John Cornwell, p.5

people. When Cardinal Richelieu (the 17th century's Adolf Hitler) finally defeated the Huguenot stronghold of La Rochelle, France, on 28 October 1628 the inhabitants were exterminated. The British Parliament had ordered her ships to the shores of the city to bring the Protestants back to England, but the Cardinal threatened that the Pope and France would declare war on England if they did. When some of these same Huguenots, who had fled to Florida and built *Fort de la Caroline* or Fort Caroline, were discovered on 28 August 1565 by a Roman Catholic military ship, they were bombarded. The surviving men were hanged, the women and children enslaved. On November 5, 1605, Guy Fawkes and a group of radical English Catholics tried to assassinate King James I and 400 members of the government by blowing up Parliament's House of Lords. On the evening of April 14, 1865 John Wilks Booth shot Abraham Lincoln, and nine hours later, Lincoln died. Booth was not only a confederate, but was part of a known group of Roman Catholics and Jesuit priests who regularly met in the area. The Vatican had a role in the perpetuation of the American Civil War, and Lincoln well knew of their involvement. To them, the government of the United States was *illegal* because their government was elected by the will of the people, not by the appointment of the Pope. Lincoln represented, to the Pope, a seat of tyranny. This is why after shooting him Booth cried out in Latin, *Sic semper tyrannis*, meaning, "Thus always to tyrants." Booth was not so much lamenting that the South had lost the war, but that the war, mostly among Protestants, was ended. You see, anyone who is not under the authority of the Pope is an enemy of his.[30]

In summary; the two titanic powers of dictatorial government/religion and republican-democracy/Protestantism were now on a collision course. The Ex Cathedra-declaration was an open defiance of the freedom and self-rule which was sweeping over Europe. Everything and almost everywhere, it seemed was going in the direction of freedom. How then could the concept of Rome's dictatorial divine authority survive? How could what Pope Boniface VIII asserted, be believed by a rational human being living in the 19th century?

We declare, assert, define and pronounce to be subject to the Roman Pontiff is to every creature altogether necessary for salvation... I have the authority of the King of Kings. I am all in all, and above all, so that God Himself and I, the Vicar of Christ, have but one consistory, and I am able to do almost all that God can do. What therefore, can you make of me but God?[31]

During that century, Rome had been exposed for what it was, and was being dismantled by virtually every European nation. Even Italy and

---

[30] https://excatholicsforchrist.com/anathema-on-the-world/
[31] Pope Boniface VIII, Papal bull Unam sanctam, 1302 A.D.

Germany, who had once formed the heart of the Holy Roman Empire, fought the Pope's claim to be the *Pontifex Maximus* going all the way back to the Tower of Babel. The most famous preacher of the 19th century, Charles Haddon Spurgeon (1834-92), pastor of the largest church in the world at the time—The Metropolitan Tabernacle, London England—would sometimes pray from his pulpit, "Oh Lord, deliver us from the Devil and the Pope!"

It was clear to many that the period between 1520 and 1800 is marked by intense persecution of Christians by totalitarian Romanism and its proxies. Had this not occurred, Europe would not only have become Protestant, but her totalitarian governments would have fallen much sooner. As it is, the Revolutions against these supposedly divinely appointed rulers did eventually come. The reign of Christ was coming to overthrow the Tower of Babel religious system.

Chapter Five

The Empire Fights Back

Going into the 20th century, the power and influence of the Vatican had suffered many significant setbacks. Yet, the *Ex-Cathedra* proclamation had only confirmed that the Office of the Pope would never give up its triple-crown claim of being the sovereign of heaven, earth and under the earth. Its desperate grasp on its remaining political strongholds increased. It claim to have supreme authority over every government was not softened—rather, its internal resolve was strengthened to an astonishingly new level. The Jesuits, who rammed through the Ex Cathedra decision issued serious threats to those leaders within Roman Catholicism who even voiced objections. This must have been bewildering to the leading nations of the world.

Years later, President Ronald Regan—in the spirit of John Wilkes—would say;

"Freedom is never more than one generation away from extinction. We didn't pass it to our children in the bloodstream. It must be fought for, protected, and handed on for them to do the same, or one day we will spend our sunset years telling our children and our children's children what it was once like in the United States where men were free."

Rome has a complex network of resources to keep itself in power and, feeling that it has a divine rite to be over the nations of the world, never lets up on that pursuit. Rome, therefore, is always involved in the politics of the nations. Sometimes it is overt, but usually it is intentionally silent, deadly silent, even, when exposed.

Preparing for the 20th century;

Before I begin discussing the World Wars that were to come, we must briefly identify what gave Rome the confidence to think that it could emerge victorious over its pursuers of the previous century.

As powerful as Europe and England were in the 19th century, no one could overlook the rise of four other countries; Canada, Australia, New Zealand, and of course, the United States of America. The economies of these nations rivaled that of Europe, in addition to being strong allies of Great Britain (as well as Holland and Switzerland). What eventually brought these five nations together even closer is their Protestantism. After WW2, they would make an alliance called, *The Five Eyes*.

Worse yet for Rome, the 19th century also saw almost a complete end to the persecutions it had used to oppose and suppress the spread of Protestantism for the previous 280 years—back to 1530. By ending the Inquisition in 1806, Napoleon did Protestantism a great service, though his goal was only to give to Europe the freedom enjoyed by the Protestant nations.

Yet, as we have seen, Romanism will never, ever, give up the pursuit of power, or the goal to re-establish that ancient Babylonian totalitarian dream. Throughout the 19th century—beginning soon after it became a nation—European elite had been trying to gain a foothold over America's banking system, and even over their money supply.[32] Control of money is the heart of the power of nations. As Benjamin Franklin asserted, "Give me control of a nation's money supply, and I could not care less who makes its laws." This is something that the man who started the Rothschild banking family, Mayer Amschel Rothschild, remarked, quoting Franklin.

Trouble was, the Constitution was in the Rothschild family's way, which says;

No State shall enter into any Treaty, Alliance, or Confederation; grant Letters of Marque and Reprisal; coin Money; emit Bills of Credit; make any Thing but gold and silver Coin a Tender in Payment of Debts; pass any Bill of Attainder, ex post facto Law, or Law impairing the Obligation of Contracts, or grant any Title of Nobility. (Art.1 sect.10 par.1)

This meant that one of the primary links binding the various States which composed the United States of America, was its money supply. Therefore, control the money supply; and you control all the States which comprise America.

When the founders drew up the Constitution for the republic, having fled the millennia-old oppressions in Europe, they ensured that only elected officials had the right to print money, not secret banking families, nor the Vatican bankers. Congress is appointed...,

To coin Money, regulate the Value thereof, and of foreign Coin, and fix the Standard of Weights and Measures, (Art.1 Sec.8 par.5)

Yet, since its inception, America's monetary system could not seem to find a stable footing. It kept crashing and struggling. The secret world of the banking elites of Europe, watching what was emerging in America, could not risk this threat to their power. So, they were—quietly—seeking to

---

[32] On the history of the Federal Reserve being used for totalitarianism, see *The Creature from Jekyll Island*, by G. Edward Griffin. From 1836-1914 America suffered seven bank crises, and only one (1819) before that. Many documentaries trace the European attempts to control the emerging USA via its currency.

get a foothold in the rising power of the United States. And America was not unaware of this threat. Several western US States banned the bankers. Populist preacher William Jennings Bryan was thrice the Democratic nominee for President from 1896 -1908. The central theme of his anti-imperialist campaign was that America was falling into a trap of "financial servitude to British capital." By that, he meant bankers.

Never-the-less, very late into the night, just before Congress closed for Christmas, on 23 December, after most of those who make America's laws were gone home, the banking elites got their chance, and they took it.

What happened on 23 December 1913 happened quietly, but it would shake the whole world for more than 100 years to come. All America woke the next morning with dismay at the discovery of what had happened that night.[33] Using the crash of 1907 as justification, a secret meeting had been held at the J.P. Morgan Estate of all the principal players in the US banking system of the time. They came up with the idea of a central bank for America, a responsibility which the Constitution stated belonged to the Congress of the United States alone. It was not established by normal legal means, but suddenly, without discussion and debate, late at night, when only barely enough Congress members were present to pass it. Just before the Christmas break was about to start, it was rushed through Congress.

When the 1913 Federal Reserve Act was passed, it gave 12 Federal Reserve Banks the ability to print money at their own discretion. Many forces within the public and government had already been calling for such a system to be put in place, so it was not a new idea. But it was only a select group who supported it. The American public was outraged when they discovered what had happened; private banks had been given control over the very heart of America's economy. Worse yet, many of those who had the keys to those banks were from Europe. Worse still, many of these banking families were deeply intertwined with the Vatican. President Woodrow Wilson, pressured by Wall Street banks, signed the Federal Reserve Act into Law, an action both the government and the people would deeply regret.

Despite its name, the Federal Reserve has nothing to do with the US Federal government. The eight families who owned what came to be known as the Fed, are the Goldman Sachs, the Rockefeller family, the Lehmans and Kuhn Loebs of New York, the Rothschilds of Paris and London, the Warburgs of Hamburg, Germany, the Lazards of Paris, and the Israel Moses Seifs of Rome. Many of the bank's stockholders reside in Europe. They finally got what they were seeking for over a century: a serious foothold of

---

[33] For a detailed account of the nefarious formation of the Federal Reserve, see; *The Creature From Jekyll Island,* by G. Edward Griffin

control in the Americas. Even before the formation of the Fed, there was a long history of financial cooperation between all these parties. Most of these families had close ties with the European royalty (having been installed to their thrones by the Vatican). Over the years these families have intermarried, strengthening these banking-monarchy ties.

Subsequent years after the Fed was established, far worse rollercoasters were seen for Americans and the world than if private bankers had not been given this control. Consider the following:

- 1914 (only one year after the Fed was established) another European war was ensued, known as The Great War. The banking cartel profited immensely from this war.

- When the war was over, the 1919 Paris Peace Conference would be presided over, ironically, by the banker, J.P. Morgan.

- After the war in Europe, America's economy was plunged into a deep crisis called The Depression of 1920-21. In real terms this was twice as serious as the Great Recession of 2007-08; 8.7% compared to 4.3%; industrial production fell 31.6% compared to 16.6%. Wrote one contemporary, "The debacle of 1920-21 was without parallel."

- The Fed flooded the US economy with easy money after the crisis of 1920-21, which created The Roaring Twenties.

- The Roaring Twenties ended with cries of despair when in 1929 a great crash decimated the US Stock Exchange. The Fed, from 1930-33, completely ended the party of the Roaring Twenties by removing 1/3 of the money supply in America! The Federal government of the most powerful country in the world could do little to chart a course out of a 10-year long Depression for its citizens. They were now owned by the European bankers.

- In the 1930's Populism resurfaced in America after it was discovered that Goldman Sachs, Lehman Bank and others profited from the Crash of 1929, when so many had been devastated.

- In his book, *The Plot to Seize the White House,* Jules Archer tells how in 1933 the Wall Street banking cartels were plotting a Fascist takeover of the White House. A 2007 BBC investigation alleged that Prescott Bush, the father and grandfather of future US presidents, was a 'key liaison' between the business plotters and the Nazi regime in Germany. Bush owed much of his wealth to his relationship with the Rockefellers. He was also a Bonesmen.

- The Great Depression was followed by another very serious war.

But not just any war, another European war, where most of America's bankers lived. The bankers, it would be discovered, were funding both sides. They had already profited from the British Boer War and the Franco-Prussian wars. They understood war for the lucrative business it could be.[34]

- After the war, The House of Morgan representatives met with the German Nazi Hjalmer Schacht at the Bank of International Settlements (BIS) in Basel, Switzerland. The House of Rockefeller BIS is the most powerful bank in the world, a global central bank for the Eight Families who control the private central banks of almost all Western and developing nations.

- Finally, from July 1-22, 1944 the Bretton Woods Agreement was signed by the 44 countries which by the end of the war made up the Allied forces of the war (though most of the war was fought by The Five Eyes countries). This commenced new monetary institutions: The World Bank and the International Monetary Fund (IMF). The bankers who funded both sides of the war, and profited immensely from it yet again – most of who were from continental Europe – saw to it that Britain and America would pay for the reconstruction of Europe!

The power of these families only grew after WW2;

The Four Horsemen of Banking (Bank of America, JP Morgan Chase, Citigroup and Wells Fargo) own the Four Horsemen of Oil (Exxon Mobil, Royal Dutch/Shell, BP and Chevron Texaco); in tandem with Deutsche Bank, BNP, Barclays and other European old money behemoths.

Companies under Rockefeller control include Exxon Mobil, Chevron Texaco, BP Amoco, Marathon Oil, Freeport McMoran, Quaker Oats, ASARCO, United, Delta, Northwest, ITT, International Harvester, Xerox, Boeing, Westinghouse, Hewlett-Packard, Honeywell, International Paper, Pfizer, Motorola, Monsanto, Union Carbide and General Foods.[35]

This brings us to the Rothschild family and the incredible power they wield. The primary repository of the wealth of this global oligarchy is the US Trust Corporation – founded in 1853 and now owned by the Bank of America. A recent US Trust Corporate Director and Honorary Trustee was Walter Rothschild. The Rothschild family has emerged as the predominant influence over global banking.

The Rothschild family, along with all the other bankers, are closely intertwined with the Vatican. When the Club of Rome was formed in 1968,

---

[34] See the book; *All Wars Are Bankers' Wars*, by Michael Rivero
[35] See *The Four Horsemen of Banking*, by Dean Henderson.

it was held at the Rothschild Estate in Accademia dei Lincei in Rome, Italy. The one entity which binds all these families together is that they are either Roman Catholic, or have kissed the Pope's ring.

Once the Federal Reserve owners (who were closely linked to the Vatican) had control of America's banking system through a Central Bank, in 1913, the way was cleared for war to occur on a serious level, as Jeffrey Tucker of the Brownstone Institute wrote;

It's highly doubtful that there ever would have been a thing called a "world war"—grotesquely called the Great War at the time—had both Europe and the United States not adopted central banks. The monetary math wouldn't have made it possible. They would have chosen diplomacy over war.

Chapter Six
World Wars; Religious Wars

A primary example of Rome's comeback from the reduction of its prestige and power in the 19th century, is its central role in bringing about WW1 personally and through the bankers. It was their negotiations around the Serbian Concordat which foolishly pitted the Austro-Hungarian empire against the Serbian empire. When Archduke Ferdinand and his wife were gunned down, precipitated by tensions during the papal negotiations, it "threw [the pope] into a profound depression from which he never recovered. He died on August 20, 1914—of a broken heart, it was said."[36]

Yet it is necessary and critical for the proper understanding of the initiating events of WW2 to note that the principal negotiator of the Serbian Concordat was a Catholic priest; Eugenio Pacelli. He would soon become the highest ranking Roman Catholic leader in Germany, and in 1939, become Pope. He would be Adolf Hitler's closest ally and supporter during his rise to power. It was Pacelli who called Germany's humiliating defeat in WW1 an "opportunity" for Germany, a Catholic Germany, to rise again—greater than ever before. It was Pacelli who prayed for Hitler, and thanked God when he survived assassination attempts on his life. For him, he stated, Hitler was, "The Saviour of Europe."

As the book, *Hitler's Pope*, and many other books make clear, it was another Concordat which Pacelli signed with the Nazis that cleared the way of their pursuit of unhindered power. It was Catholics in both Germany and Italy[37] who would join the "centralization of power" in these countries because they believed it had the Pope's blessing. We would likely never have heard of Adolf Hitler and the Third Reich had it not been for the political ambitions of the Vatican and Pacelli's personal commitment to total dictatorship over Catholicism—a commitment that was higher than even that of the Fuhrer.[38]

---

[36] Cornwell, p.58.

[37] See the ward winning book, *The Pope And Mussolini: The Secret History Of Pius XI And The Rise Of Fascism In Europe,* by David Kertzer

[38] Cornwell writes in the. Vanity Fair article; "Pacelli's coronation was the most triumphalist in a hundred years. His style of papacy, for all his personal humility, was unprecedentedly pompous. He always ate alone. Vatican bureaucrats were obliged to take phone calls from him on their knees. When he took his afternoon walk, the gardeners had to hide in the bushes. Senior

Pause for a moment and ask a few questions about the Second World War, and you will realize that the Pope and Hitler were uncomfortable, on-and-off again, bed-fellows. Where does the term *"Heil Hitler"* find its roots, except in the first Roman Empire; *Hail Caesar*? Wasn't *the Nazi Salute* always known as *The Roman Salute* before this (the salute they used as the general greeting between those attending the trial of Martin Luther at the Diet of Worms, for example)? Wasn't the Nazi Cross (Swastika) commonly displayed as artwork in the Vatican long before WW2, and a symbol of its religion? Why was it called the *Third* Reich, which would last *a thousand years*? (Internet sites will tell you the first Reich and second Reich were various German empires, and some will even list the Holy Roman Empire as the first. But the fact is that both previous Roman Empires lasted almost exactly 1,000-years, and are the only reigns in the history of the world which lasted that long.) It only makes sense that the alliance of Germany-Italy-Bosnia (Spain and Portugal remained neutral, but allowed soldiers to join the Nazi invasion of Russia; being Fascist governments who "would not take a side"). Was not Benito Mussolini openly stating that he was beginning a new Roman Empire? Why did Hitler base the Code of Discipline for the infamous *"SS"* on that of the Jesuit's Code of Discipline? It has been estimated that half of Hitler's "SS" were former RC priests.[39] Why did the governments of Germany, Italy and (Catholic) Croatia[40] all become totalitarian, like the Vatican is, for the war? For most of the war the conflict did not involve *all* the nations of the world. Truth is, the enemies of the Axis powers were Britain, Canada, Australia, and New Zealand, and finally, the United States—that is, the five predominantly Protestant nations of the world outside of Western Europe.

Most importantly, it needs to be pointed out that all the predominantly Roman Catholic nations of the world would not oppose the Axis Powers but remained neutral. But even this neutrality was secured only after, according to the book *A Man Called Intrepid* by William Stevenson, they were pressured by the American and British governments. In the first year of the war, Roman Catholic South America and Mexico were actively supplying and supporting the German Nazi and Italian Fascist governments by providing safe ports and resupply for their ships. According to Stevenson, who was the head of Secret Intelligence for the Allies, if Brazil did not stop supporting the Axis war effort by subversion efforts (which were successful), both America (before they had declared war on Germany and

---

officials were not allowed to ask him questions or present a point of view." The Pope of Hitler's day was as dictatorial as Hitler.

[39] See; *Hitler's Priests; Catholic Clergy and National Socialism*, by Kevin Spicer

[40] The horrific crimes of the *Ushashi* men like Pavelic against Serbian Orthodox Christians even prompted the Nazi SS to step in to stop them. Pavelic, the very next month, was a guest of Pacelli at the Vatican!

Italy) and Britain were going to bomb their cities.[41]

Finally, it is noteworthy that the Mexican and South American nation's official enlistment of support for the Allies only began when the Italian government fell in July 1943, and the Allies captured the city of Rome in June 1944.[42] The dates speak for themselves, and it is astonishing to see a timeline chart of the various dates' world nations joined the Allies. Even Ireland and the province of Quebec in Canada, would not assist the Allies until after it was clear that the war could not be won by the Axis Powers; after Rome was defeated. Knowing what we do about the origins of Islam, it is not surprising that the Muslim nations were sympathetic to the Nazis as well, and did not aid the Allies until after Rome was conquered.[43]

Furthermore, the reason America hesitated to join the war is quite revealing as related by Stevenson, who would have had inside knowledge due to the Allies' spy network. The American Ambassador to Great Britain was Joseph F. Kennedy. Due to his position, Kennedy was aware of secret movements within the Allied war effort. Almost from the beginning of the war Scotland Yard was viewing him as an information leak for both the Nazis, and to Rome specifically. On Kennedy's vacation back to America he openly talked about how he believed the war effort to save Great Britain from the Nazis was hopeless, and that he had been telling the British government this along with his ambitions to run for the US presidency. He had been telling President Roosevelt to "trust" Hitler. To Churchill, "he had consistently explained away Germany's step-by-step conquest of Europe" (ch.13). An Allied informant in Rome said that even private communications between the US President and the PM of Britain were being relayed back to "Rome" and "the German Ambassador to Italy." The "informant" had to be Kennedy, but no one had the nerve to confront the US Ambassador. When Japan invaded China, the incredible losses of life were "unavoidable" according to Kennedy, and "was regretted by no one more than the Japanese." A few days after Britain declared war on Germany, Kennedy put on a dinner for his family, where he toasted the Germans who "would badly thrash the British."

For some time after the war started, Churchill and Roosevelt distrusted

---

[41] *A Man Called Intrepid*, William Stevenson, Ch. 32.

[42] Argentina, Mar. 1945; Bolivia, Apr. 1943; Brazil Aug. 1942 (bribed with a US Air Base); Chile, Apr. 45; Columbia, July 1943; Mexico, May 1942 (threatened by the US); Peru, Feb. 1945.

[43] Egypt, Feb. 1945; Iran, Sept. 1943; Iraq, Jan. 1943 (though it fought against Britain); Saudi Arabia, Mar. 1945; Syria Feb 1945; Turkey, Feb 1945 (it had entered into a "Friendship Agreement" with the Nazis in 1941). Oman is the exception, Sept. 1939. Many remained "neutral." (https://worldpopulationreview.com)

each other. It was not until Churchill, in frustration, paid a personal visit to the US President that the reason for their mistaken impression of each other came to light. Joseph Kennedy had been misinforming them about the other's intentions, intentionally creating suspicion between them. During a personal visit, Kennedy's presence was not needed, and the truth came out, whereupon Churchill went into a "deadly attack" on Ambassador Kennedy. Many wondered why Kennedy was not executed for treason.

Joseph Kennedy openly voiced Roman Catholic sympathies generally, along with an open support of Hitler's Nazism before the war. Reading *Intrepid* it is clear that he engaged in subterfuge within the Allied countries as they sought to organize opposition to the Axis Powers once war was declared. While this is not the primary focus of Stevenson's book, and I have only listed a few points about him, clearly this was the case. From the Index of Subjects at the back of the text are listed all the references to these verified activities of Kennedy. Reading them leads to only one conclusion: Kennedy's "defeatist influence" within Britain and America, specifically as a Roman Catholic with connections to Rome, greatly hampered the Allies' opposition to the Axis forces.

Victims of the Axis Powers left vulnerable due to "well-positioned Papal allies" was vast, and could not be measured. Of note, the vast majority of lay Roman Catholics are unaware of such papal machinations. For example, after WW1, practically all of Europe and Great Britain had its citizens (including those Roman Catholic) stripped of their personal means of self-protection (armaments). This was sold as being essential to "never let a war like that happen again". That this was a primary enabler for the Nazi's rapid success when its armies rolled over Europe should raise suspicion. Only a Totalitarian government, or a want-to-be one, would disarm its law-abiding citizens. A Republican government would *want* law-abiding citizens armed, for fear of a totalitarian one. Could it be that it was men like Kennedy, strategically placed, who created a defenceless Europe in the years leading up to WW2? That would require investigation beyond the scope of this work.

After WW2, with over 100 million dead, Pacelli "condemned" the genocide of more than 6 million people by the Nazis. The Allied Powers openly stated that his apology for Rome's role in the Holocaust was "inadequate." Rome, on the other hand, remained unrepentant. Like the defiant declaration of 1870 at Vatican I; *ex Cathedra,* the next pope began the process of declaring Pope Pacelli a Saint at the final session of Vatican II. He was then declared a *Servant of God* (the first step toward official sainthood) by pope John Paul II, and in 2009 pope Benedict XVI declared him *Venerable* (the next step). Hitler's Pope[44] is on his way to becoming a Saint!

The Second World War was a war of political ideology. Totalitarianism (Nazism, Fascism, the dictator of Spain, Empiricism in Japan) against the constitutional republican-democracies. It was a war against freedom of thought and speech. It was the religion of the Tower of Babel trying once again to gain supreme control of the world.

The pope who ruled during WW2 spent the rest of his life traveling around the world on good-will tours. He is the most-traveled pope in history. His efforts were likely that the Vatican would not be held accountable for what they had done, again, in their effort to make the seat of the pope – the Pontifex Maximus—what it claimed to be: supreme ruler of Heaven and Earth and the Underworld. Two World Wars, hundreds of millions of dead, all to fulfil their age-old dream of ultimate and unrestricted power.[45]

---

[44] A fitting title, when one reads the book by that title by, John Cornwell, or a summary article of it in *Vanity Fair* with the same title; Long-Buried Vatican Files Reveal A New Indictment Of Pope Pius XII | *Vanity Fair*

[45] It is common for people to believe this connection was insignificant, but the introduction to the Jesuit Oath, on which the *SS* was built, makes clear how the Vatican feels about governments not under their control:

I, _____ now, in the presence of Almighty God, the Blessed Virgin Mary, the blessed Michael the Archangel, the blessed St. John the Baptist, the holy Apostles St. Peter and St. Paul and all the saints and sacred hosts of heaven, and to you, my ghostly father, the Superior General of the Society of Jesus, founded by St. Ignatius Loyola in the Pontificate of Paul the Third, and continued to the present, do by the womb of the virgin, the matrix of God, and the rod of Jesus Christ, declare and swear, that his holiness the Pope is Christ's Vice-regent and is the true and only head of the Catholic or Universal Church throughout the earth; and that by virtue of the keys of binding and loosing, given to his Holiness by my Savior, Jesus Christ, he hath power to depose heretical kings, princes, states, commonwealths and governments, all being illegal without his sacred confirmation and that they may safely be destroyed. Therefore, to the utmost of my power I shall and will defend this doctrine of his Holiness' right and custom against all usurpers of the heretical or Protestant authority whatever, especially the Lutheran of Germany, Holland, Denmark, Sweden, Norway, and the now pretended authority and churches of England and Scotland, and branches of the same now established in Ireland and on the Continent of America and elsewhere; and all adherents in regard that they be usurped and heretical, opposing the sacred Mother Church of Rome. I do now renounce and disown any allegiance as due to any heretical king, prince or state named Protestants or Liberals, or obedience to any of the laws, magistrates or

Pope Pius XII would eventually go to his grave, but not peacefully. For the last three years of his life, he was overtaken by the most horrible night-terrors. His caretakers report that through-out the papal apartments one could hear each night the blood-curdling screaming of Pius. These night-terrors of the supposed-vicar of Christ were occurring during sleep, when one can no longer hide what was truly going on in their mind. Surely the national leaders knew what the Vatican had done in supporting Nazism; that Rome had intended to establish International Fascism on the world. Pacelli himself, according to John Cornwall—perhaps the world's leading expert on Pacelli— was passionate about establishing the "dictatorial authority" of the Papacy on the world.[46] If world leaders had spoken—if they had explained to the world why before attacking Germany, they had to capture the city of Rome—then the Roman religion, the New Babylon, Nimrod's 4,000-year-old dream, would surely have been finished. But for the most part, they took the secret with them to the grave.[47]

---

officers....I furthermore promise and declare that I will, when opportunity present, make and wage relentless war, secretly or openly, against all heretics, Protestants and Liberals, as I am directed to do, to extirpate and exterminate them from the face of the whole earth; and that I will spare neither age, sex or condition; and that I will hang, waste, boil, flay, strangle and bury alive these infamous heretics, rip up the stomachs and wombs of their women and crush their infants' heads against the walls, in order to annihilate forever their execrable race. That when the same cannot be done openly, I will secretly use the poisoned cup, the strangulating cord, the steel of the poniard or the leaden bullet, regardless of the honor, rank, dignity, or authority of the person or persons, whatever may be their condition in life, either public or private, as I at any time may be directed so to do by any agent of the Pope or Superior of the Brotherhood of the Holy Faith, of the Society of Jesus.

[46] *"But there was another side to [Pacelli's] character, little known to the faithful. Although he was a man of selfless, monk-like habits of prayer and simplicity, he was a believer in the absolute-leadership principle. More than any other Vatican official of the century, he had promoted the modern ideology of autocratic papal control, the highly centralized, dictatorial authority he himself assumed on March 2, 1939, and maintained until his death in October 1958."* Long-Buried Vatican Files Reveal A New Indictment Of Pope Pius XII | *Vanity Fair*

[47] An excellent website for this kind of information is www.excatholicsforchrist.com

Chapter Seven
One Last Time

Pacelli died in 1958. It must have seemed to the Vatican by then that they were not going to be held accountable for their part in WW2. One would think that what would follow would be a 1,000-year reign of humility and repentance by the Vatican. But when an entity sees itself as having divine authority to rule the world, when it is the inheritor of the spiritual forces behind the Tower of Babel, world wars can be categorized as mere setbacks.

The goal to see Papal powers achieve world dominance now took on a new direction, that of a war of infiltration and subversion.

The Vatican II sessions were convened from October 1962 to December 1965. These meetings were intended to project the message that Rome had changed. She was a humbler and more conciliatory empire. The Mass was no longer said in Latin, but in the language of the people. Luther had said the Bible should be in the language of the people, Rome seemed now to agree. She sought to have discussions with Protestant denominations (dialogue, they called it. Surely this could not be offensive to Protestants?), and did not openly oppose Democracy anymore.

The process of bringing Europe together under one government began soon after WW2. In 1957, two primary treaties were signed which began the Unification of Europe: The European Economic Community (EEC) Treaty and the European Atomic Energy Community (Euratom). Together, they were ironically named, *The Treaty of Rome*.

Then there is the new European flag. The EU flag was adopted in 1955, and set the stage for Europe's future. Roman Catholic spokesmen consistently deny that the EU flag has anything to do with the religion of Romanism and the formation of the EU being the achievement of a Roman Catholic European state. They attempt to deny that the flag has any theological significance, even though its two creators were devoutly Roman Catholic.

If this flag is not the brain-child of the Vatican, how can the blue colour—same as that which is traditionally used as vestments for the Virgin Mary in Roman Catholic art in the Vatican—be explained? What explains the twelve stars, in the same crown-shape, as those depicted on

Vatican statues and paintings of their Virgin Mary? Is this not the very picture of the "woman" of Revelation 12:1, "A great and wondrous sign appeared in heaven: a woman clothed with the sun, with the moon under her feet and a crown of twelve stars on her head."? Arsène Heitz, one of the designers of the flag said that he intended the connection between "The Blessed Virgin and the Queen of the Apocalypse." He also noted the date of the flag's adoption was significant too; December 8, 1955, coinciding with the Catholic Feast of the Immaculate Conception of the Blessed Virgin Mary. One cannot reasonably deny that the primary roots of the European Union are firmly imbedded in restoring Western Europe to the realm long sought-after by the one who sits in the seat of ancient Roman authority.

The European Union, after further treaties and agreements, in 1992, was officially formed via the Maastricht Treaty.

The point is this: is not the EU the very establishment desired by the Axis powers and Pope Pius XII in the first place? Did they not want a unified Europe, with the Vatican as the chief religious center? Did they not want it run by an unelected body, appointed from within, most of whom are former employees of the Vatican? And is it not a socialist dream, perfectly in line with the intentions of the Axis Powers—perfectly in line with the Vatican's own doctrine of Distributism?

Having now consumed Western Europe, these intentions continue to incorporate the remaining territories and countries of what used to compose The Holy Roman Empire, which would include much of Eastern Europe.

Then the Vatican moved beyond its European ambitions to form a world-wide coordinating body to spread what it had achieved via the European Union to the rest of the nations; The Club of Rome. It is this (obviously Roman Catholic) organization that set forth a globalist agenda.

The first Club of Rome meeting was held in 1968, at the Rockefeller mansion (its banking partner). This meeting made it clear that the Vatican II meetings were no more than lipstick on a pig. The Club of Rome meeting adopted a new tactic. It did not involve armies directly, for it saw that this failed over time. Rather, it sought to use seduction and subversion. The goal became to destabilize, demoralize, and deconstruct their foes from within their own nations. This would be done on a global level, but the focus would be on the five nations who had defeated the Axis powers.

The Daily Coin, on January 3, 2021 published the origins of the

Globalist Plan for the future. The Club of Rome openly stated how they would sell it to the public:

The next decisive step toward the global economic transformation was taken with the first report of the Club of Rome.

In 1968, the Club of Rome was initiated at the Rockefeller estate Bellagio in Italy. Its first report was published in 1972 under the title *"The Limits to Growth."*

The president emeritus of the Club of Rome, Alexander King, and the secretary of the club, General Bertrand Schneider, inform in their *Report to the Council of Rome* that when the members of the club were in search of identifying a new enemy, they listed pollution, global warming, water shortages, and famines as the most opportune items to be blamed on humanity with the implication that humanity itself must be reduced to keep these threats in check.

"In searching for a new enemy to unite us, we came up with the idea that pollution, the threat of global warming, water shortages, famine and the like would fit the bill. All these dangers are caused by human intervention, and it is only through changed attitudes and behavior that they can be overcome. The real enemy then, is humanity itself."

The goal of the Club of Rome was to turn humanity upon itself that it might self-destruct. This form of national suicide would leave a gaping power-hole to fill. This would be done from a multitude of directions, seemingly disconnected from each other. Yet every method would have the same goal: ruining the world which did not submit to the one who thought he should be king of heaven, earth, and the world under the earth.[48] As the Jesuit saying goes, "It is better to rule a country ruined, than rule a country heathen [non-Roman Catholic]."

After all, as Pope Frances recently stated, *"We define that the Holy Apostolic See and the Roman Pontiff hold primacy over the whole world."*

I will now briefly list examples of how this is being done, using the Allied country I know best as the readiest example.

---

[48] See; https://excatholicsforchrist.com/anathema-on-the-world/

Chapter Eight
A Beast with Ten Horns and Seven Heads

When the Bible describes the revived Babylonian Empire, it says that "it has seven heads and ten horns" (Rev. 12:3; 13:1; 17:3, see also, Dan. 7:7, 20). The meaning of this reference is varied and debated, as there are a variety of possible meanings. In fact, there are likely layers to this concept.

One of the ways to understand it is to see that this final kingdom will not have only one "face," but a whole variety of them—a whole variety of ways that it can be examined and understood. All of them are true faces, even if they do not agree with each other and even at times are in a state of serious conflict with each other. The point is that they are all attached to the same beast, and have but one end in mind: the supreme authority of the Beast.

Not to understand that this truth behind Romanism is to be vulnerable to one of its most effective machinations; Roman Catholicism can be whatever you want it to be. You just need to find the head that pleases you, be it God, Allah, Brahmin, nirvana, Atheism, power, poverty, or wealth, social services, fill in the blank. Its support and application of the Theory of Evolution to the educational institutions of the Western world is a perfect example.

Promoter of Evolution

It should be clear that Romanism is the wielder of the Theory of Evolution. However, if most Evolutionists are also Atheists, how can they have anything to do with Roman Catholicism? Just as nations use mercenaries in times of war, so Rome uses those who assist in their over-all goals. Rome has plenty of room for Atheism within its ranks.

Not all that long ago Roman Catholics were not allowed to have Bibles, and Protestants who possessed them (especially in Europe) were burned along with their Bibles.

"No one may possess the books of the Old and New Testaments in the Romance language (such as French, Italian, Spanish, etc.), and if anyone possesses them he must turn them over to the local bishop within eight days after the promulgation of this decree, so that they may be burned."[49]

As we have already noted above, the middle of the 19th century saw the

---

[49] Council of Tarragona, the Roman Catholic Church Council of 1234 A.D.

Vatican lose a great deal of its influence. But just as Rome claims to be the *Eternal City,* so it will never admit defeat. Never. When Charles Darwin published *The Origin of the Species* in 1859, Rome saw in it an opportunity to attack the Bible's premises and authority, since burning it was no longer a politically expedient option.

Some may question this, but I have on my shelf a book titled *Reformation,* published by a Roman Catholic in 1888. Already the Vatican had so adopted the Theory of Evolution that the author states the need of the Church to *apologize* for having believed anything contrary to it. By 1874, RC priests had taken sides within the theory's internal debates, such as the one between Ernst Haeckel and Darwin, who was aligned with Bismarck against Haeckel's charts. They did not question if Evolution was true, but rather how it happened. Rome makes no effort to defend the Bible's view of the creation of the universe, but will happily employ those who argue against the Bible on this most fundamental point.

Then, with Germany leading the way in the promotion of Evolutionary fervor among her intellectuals, much of their population was supportive of the concept that human races were to be ranked as being further or lesser developed along the Evolutionary chain. It was a small step from there to convince the population that the Arian race was the most superior of all the five races postulated. This easily led to the extermination of millions of "lower" peoples in order to keep the higher one pure and to clear the way for it to advance. Not only did Rome not oppose this, but actively supported both the theory and the racial purification principle. The Theory of Evolution proved to be an effective tool in de-humanizing other humans. Eugenics, which arises out of the Theory of Evolution, created a scientific justification for German soldiers to eliminate so called "lower races" as though they were sub-human. In the late 1800s, German soldiers were taken to Africa to "practice" war, while at the same time furthering the purity of humanity. This same intent was enacted to justify the elimination of "lower races" in the Nazi Concentration Camps. The Vatican was not only supportive of the concept of this purifying, but also of the Theory which justified it.

While it has become common for people to think of Nazism as "right wing," it is the opposite which is true, as Brendan Simms's book, *Hitler: A Global Biography* convincingly argues. Nazism was primarily anti-Capitalist and anti-Democratic, and for this reason, feared Britain and American Anglo-Saxons. Nazism is socialism and totalitarianism, like Fascist Italy and Communist Russia, Spain, Croatia and others who sided with them. They were all socialist and totalitarian; "left wing." Look at what is going on in the USA today and the way Donald Trump is treated on all sides from the media to the politicians: it is the totalitarian sympathizers who see him for the threat he poses to the new world order. They are from "the Left." The integration of Evolution into halls of academia and every-day understanding is but a tool for Racism to propagate in new forms.

It must be stated that this is the same justification used in abortion; children in the womb are—at most—subhuman. Until good science proved that a child in the womb was indeed truly human, the argument put forward by Haeckel's embryo comparison charts were used to de-humanize in the same way as did German concentration camps. The charts were outright frauds, but even after they were proved as such, they continued to be referenced in Roman Catholic schools (such as the ones I attended). Rome would not separate itself from Evolution.

In fact, the Theory was in serious trouble due to scientific advancements which were regularly discovering just how complex life was, making it less and less likely that physical things could make themselves out of nothing. Especially when it was confirmed that dirt and water (from which everything is made) could not think, plan or develop themselves. But to the rescue came Georges Henri Joseph Édouard Lemaître. With a Jesuit education, Lemaître eventually joined the ultra-secret Society. During the 1930s he continually spread his theory, and while there were many objectors who saw significant problems with it, it eventually caught on in spite of the fact that, "Einstein thought it unjustifiable from a physical point of view." But as the saying goes, "If you repeat something often enough, people will eventually believe it." Lemaître was showered with opportunities to speak, and was made a professor at *The Catholic University of America*, was made an honorary canon of the Malines, and became a member of the *Pontifical Academy of Sciences*. The Theory of Evolution was thus saved by a RC priest, though significant numbers of scientists still openly doubt it.[50] This leads into their role in bringing forward abortion to Western societies, based upon Evolutionary theory.

For the most part, I only know Roman Catholicism's role in abortion as it happened in Canada. Its role cannot be described as anything less than highly duplicitous. After the Club of Rome meeting in 1968 mentioned above, Canada's news media did all it could to promote the rise of a new kind of politician, and that to the office of Prime Minister; one who was *progressive*. Pierre Elliot Trudeau was just the kind of PM someone would want if they wanted to change Canada from being the boring, highly-stable, wealthy, moral, and Protestant nation as it was known as around the world,

---

[50] An article on www.rense.com titled 'Big bang theory busted by 33 top scientists' (27 May 2004) says, 'Our ideas about the history of the universe are dominated by big bang theory. But its dominance rests more on funding decisions than on the scientific method, according to Eric Lerner, mathematician Michael Ibison of Earthtech.org, and dozens of other scientists from around the world.'

into one that was more "open." This was especially true when it came to abortion.

Pierre Trudeau was firmly Roman Catholic. He is said to have gone to Mass every day. Therefore, Rome's agenda was his own, and his own was Rome's. What was good for Canada, was in Trudeau's opinion, what was Roman Catholic. Morally and sexually, he was completely out of synch with most Canadians, yet it was in line with his progressiveness and the Priests. He was sexually uninhibited in the extreme, even while married. According to his bodyguards, he was constantly slipping away for a sexual experience with someone (Many believe that his son, Justin, is the son of Cuban president, Castro, and the resemblance makes this more than a theory. Pierre and his wife, Margaret, were visiting the dictator at the right time for it to be true).

Trudeau Sr. did not simply make abortion legal in Canada, he went further. All laws against it were completely removed. There are simply no laws against it in Canada. His "science" was based upon the Theory of Evolution, and the media in Canada backed him almost without question.

Did his Catholicism get in the way of this? The answer is that Rome was for the most part silent about Trudeau's abortion policies in Canada. There were some deviant priests who voiced objections (see the "10 heads" point above), but none of it went anywhere. In fact, Romanism, like always, played both sides of the fence. On the one hand, they would not criticize their man for making it permissible in Canada. On the other hand, their low-level priests bemoaned it as a practice forbidden for Catholics. They protested it, and set up workshops to combat it in their midst, among Catholics, and for those who attended their Mass (in my Catholic school I heard this too). But Trudeau continued to go to Mass every day, continued to get the support of the RC media, and when he finally died, was given a funeral "fit for a king" by a Bishop, as the newspapers proudly proclaimed.

What are we to make of this duplicity? The same thing we are to think of what was going on in Nazi Germany. The Arian Race was promoting high birthrates among their own, while at the same time eliminating by extermination those who were not. Abortion accomplishes the same thing: among Catholics, all are pro-family with restricted birth control use (yes, this was discouraged for Catholic families too), while at the same time, abortion is freely available for the rest of the population. Team this up with newspaper articles bemoaning a world that was over-populated, and the logical result was that the rest of the Canadian population sought to heavily restrict their family size. Canada, steadily, was brought under the control of Rome. All the while, evidence suggests that the Vatican heavily invested in companies which produced birth control pills, and later in "the morning after" pills.

Canada went on to have a long succession of Roman Catholic Prime Ministers, none of whom would touch the abortion issue. Ironically, it was not until Steven Harper was elected as Prime Minister (almost 40 years after Trudeau had been elected) that he was hounded by the press on the issue of Abortion. Suspicions were regularly raised that he would create laws to regulate it, and readers were warned. No matter how much Harper dismissed accusations over abortion policy, they kept coming up. Once he was out of office (thanks to Canada's RC-controlled media), and was replaced by another Roman Catholic, Justin Trudeau, suddenly the abortion issue went away. Steven Harper was Canada's only Protestant PM since 1968.

I heard that in the US the president of Planned Parenthood considered himself "a Good Catholic." No surprise there; the largest supporter of abortion in America is not disciplined by the Vatican, just like in Canada!

Promotion of Senseless American Wars;

Did you know that in the Korean War, Canadian military leadership would not let its troops be commanded by Americans because they said the US wastes the lives of its men? This fact is well-known by many nations other than Canada. European troops in the Afghanistan war stayed in well-sheltered bunkers, while Canadian, Australian, and especially American troops did the fighting. But even in that conflict, the Canadian soldiers with whom I spoke were astonished at how readily American officers ordered their troops into highly dangerous situations with little hesitation. Canadian soldiers were told to step aside and let the Americans do it. When they did, they were horrified at the carnage. Those I spoke to also reflected that with a little planning, a better outcome could have been accomplished, with much less loss of life and limb. This same situation has been the case with many wars beyond the two mentioned, especially in Vietnam.

What must be understood to find the reasons behind America's senseless wars? I would posit four things;

1. Most of the fighting soldiers in the US are Republican, naturally, fighting for their nation's principles. Historically, US soldiers are those who are the most patriotic. That is commendable, but it also means that it is them who are losing life and limb, and not those who are less committed to "what America stands for in the world."

2. Most US officers are Roman Catholic, or theologically liberal. I mentioned this to a Protestant US chaplain, and at first, he balked. But then I asked him about the base where he was currently stationed. After a few moments' thought about its leadership and their values basis, his eyes widened in surprise. I told him there

must be exceptions to this trend, but that I was yet to find one. I spoke to a US Army officer who had converted to Catholicism from Protestantism about the reason he converted. He had only one reason: to enhance the possibility of his promotion.

3. Senseless wars sour not only the reputation of America, a nation known as being highly Protestant around the world, but drain the resources of that same largely Protestant nation. Who, it should be asked, stands to benefit when this is the case?

4. Senseless wars may not be completely senseless after all. The result of the Vietnam War was the immigration of large numbers of so-called "Boat People" from South Vietnam. These refugees were almost all Roman Catholics, and at the time those responsible for finding homes for them in the US government were also Roman Catholic, who also made sure that they were placed into…the homes of Roman Catholic sponsors. In the Balkans War from 1991-99, America and her allies defended the Bosnians against the Serbians. Serbia was not invaded, just bombed into submission by NATO (read: US) forces. No one brought up the fact that in WW2 the Bosnian Ustaše, the equivalent of the German "SS", had carried out a terrible genocide against the Serbs, nor that the Bosnians were "Good Catholics," while the Serbs were Orthodox. Maybe it was not so senseless after all?

Many military members join for patriotic reasons. Some may join for economic benefits. Some join to continue a family legacy of service. These are honorable reasons that commend my admiration. Many, if not most, do not realize the influence that the Roman Catholic Church has on these military institutions. The influence is so high up, spiritual, and many times compartmentalized, that the new recruit has almost no knowledge or visibility of the influence. I believe the new recruit's intentions are pure and honorable. And that is why I highlight these truths; to expose the plans that include the use of the military as a tool and hopefully open their eyes.

Your duty and your service is truly admired and appreciated. There are forces trying to use your honest efforts for their evil gain.

When it comes to the purposes of the US "military-industrial-complex" which rose after WW2, there was a great danger of the complex being used for nefarious reasons, of which President Eisenhower spoke about in his Farewell Address to the nation. In part he warned, *"In the councils of government, we must guard against the acquisition of unwarranted influence, whether sought or unsought, by the military-industrial complex. The potential for the disastrous rise of misplaced power exists and will persist."*

He was warning future leaders about is the possibility of "misplaced power" which would not look out for the interests of the American people, but of other agendas.

Crippling Debt;

Before Pierre Trudeau was elected Prime Minister in Canada, Canadians were famous for saving their money. It is said that the average Canadian saved approximately 20% of their income in the mid-1960s. This made Canada a very stable nation.

But consider what happened with the election of successive Roman Catholic Prime Ministers: With the election of Pierre Trudeau in 1969, all this changed. Canada's debt began to skyrocket. The Fraser Institute reports that 97% of Canada's current debt was accumulated after 1970, and this number does not include the stats after 2007. This time-period, with the election of Trudeau #2, saw a more than doubling of Canada's debt (as well as the sale of all of Canada's gold reserves, in his first 6 months)! It was also during this time when Canada went from its first Protestant Prime Minister in 50 years, to yet another Roman Catholic (compare that in Canada's first hundred years, there were only two RC PMs). It is worth noting that after 9 years in office, PM Harper had balanced Canada's federal books, and was about to begin paying *down* Canada's national debt. Under his leadership Canadians hardly noticed the 2008 financial crisis which rocked much of the rest of the world.

What is true about Canada's rising debt, is true of all the other Allied countries. Their debts have almost, and likely will, collapse their economies. This will create the necessity for a Great Reset.

Chapter Nine
Further Considerations

I now want to remind my readers that my goal in this paper is to be brief. I have lists of topics in front of me which refer to ways in which the Allied countries have been weakened and morally dismantled by Romanism and its allies. The detailing of them would lengthen the paper more than I want to. This, I believe, would detract from the main purpose of this paper. Reviewers of what I have written contact me about other connections they have seen since they began looking for it; "Its hiding in plain sight!" But I do not want to cite every example I can think of, as tempting as it is.

I want to get to the fact that this hatred of Donald Trump, or the essence of what he represents (republican constitutional freedoms arising from the West's Protestant heritage) is 4,000 years-old, and is reaching the crisis point. I will now leave the reader with bullet points, for which there is plenty of evidence on the internet and other academic journals or resources to see that what I am saying is true (though "someone" seems to be combing through the internet either rewriting histories or suppressing information. So be careful of your sources). Please keep in mind that these points for consideration are all connected by one theme: something that arose in the wake of the religion of Babylon is here and has been working for a long time to overthrow the Kingdom of Light with the Kingdom of Darkness. To replace freedom with tyranny.

1. Not only in Canada, but in the US, the liberalization of historically Protestant seminaries and collages (Toronto School of Theology, Calvin Seminary, Western Seminary, are but token examples) occurred as they began conciliatory "talks" with Roman Catholics. After Vatican II, Rome sought to infiltrate Protestant denominations under the guise that they had changed, and to great effect. So many seminaries are now wrestling with theological compromise and Wokeism.

2. John F. Kennedy was America's first Roman Catholic President, yet, unlike his father, he was an America-first president. This was to the surprise of Roman Catholic secret societies. On 27 April 1961, JFK gave a speech to the American Society of Newspaper Publishers Association. His warning was of secret societies which had already infiltrated the US government and were seeking to use it for their own means. While some of the speech could have been referencing international Communism, there are other aspects of it which bear the marks of an enemy which was much more

entrenched, and with whom he was much more familiar. That JFK did not name this entity as Communism, which would have been perfectly acceptable at the time, is a strong indication that he was referring to something else. The introduction to the speech contains this passage:

For we are opposed around the world by a monolithic and ruthless conspiracy that relies primarily on covert means for expanding its sphere of influence–on infiltration instead of invasion, on subversion instead of elections, on intimidation instead of free choice, on guerrillas by night instead of armies by day. It is a system which has conscripted vast human and material resources into the building of a tightly knit, highly efficient machine that combines military, diplomatic, intelligence, economic, scientific and political operations.

The fact is, Rome has so many secret societies it can be hard to keep track of them all, except by detailed charts. Logic says that surely JFK was approached at some point too by the secret societies in his own religion, especially considering the role his father played in World War II which we reviewed above.

3. Did you notice how many pro-Roman Catholic movies were produced after WW2? All of them were designed to distance Rome from its involvement in its past nefarious affairs. *Gone with the Wind* attempted to distance Romanism from its involvement in the American Civil War, by portraying them as co-victims of its miseries. While individual Roman Catholics no doubt suffered, it is also true that the organization's role in keeping the war (Protestant against Protestant) going is well documented. The shooting of Abraham Lincoln was a conspiracy of Catholic priests and loyal Catholics. It was Roman Totalitarianism sentiment behind Lincoln's assassin in his declaration, "sic semper tyrannis," which is the Virginia State motto, even to this day. Booth was from Maryland, and an ardent Catholic. Both these states are, obviously, named after the Roman Catholic themes of the Virgin Mary. Booth was part of a larger plan to assassinate all the leadership of the US government. At the time, states governed by democracy were illegal according to the Vatican. Rome was very open about its hatred of leaders elected by the people, and not appointed by the Pope. To Roman Catholic leaders, such government officials were "tyrannis" or "Tyrants." Therefore, while it was true that Roman Catholics suffered during the Civil War, Romanism hoped the war would destroy the whole of this "illegal" US government structure, and that is why Booth and his supporters wanted the war to continue; it was this that *Gone with the Wind* hoped to cover up. Movies that were produced to the same end were *The Sound of*

Music, which portrayed the Austrian people as being anti-Nazi. This was far from true, and letters read by their RC Bishops to the congregations did much to swell support for it. Some books to further consult on this topic: *The Pope At War: The Secret History of Pope Pius XII, Mussolini, and Hitler;* and *Hitler's Pope.* Be aware that the Vatican has commissioned writers to counter these books, as well as loaded the internet with rewritten histories to cover its past. A friend of mine, a Ph.D. student attending a Roman Catholic University, was approached to help with this for a summer job.

4. On the topic of movies, it is important to point out that there has become a coalition of parties who have a vested interest in tearing down the foundations over Western society. Modern constitutional-republican nations were established by Protestants in general, and continental Reformed/Scottish Presbyterians in particular.[51] If it were not for them, we would have returned to the Dark Ages. This success dismantled the power of Totalitarianism. Therefore, Babylon will align with whatever support can be mustered against what this newfound freedom built. This is why practically everyone in Hollywood is Roman Catholic, Jewish, or a whole variety of various religions, including a powerful element of Satanists and those involved in the Occult and Witchcraft.[52] All reject Christ as the only way, truth, and life, (John 14:6) and their shared goal is the re-shaping of the American world view; and the corruption of its Christian morality.

Have you ever noticed how many times in movies using the name of *Jesus* is used in a in a blasphemous way? It happens quite often. A perfect example is in the movie, *The Princess Bride,* with Robert Reiner as director. Robert Reiner is Jewish. The blasphemy of the name of *Jesus*

---

[51] See, *How the Scots Invented the Modern World: The True Story of How Western Europe's Poorest Nation Created Our World and Everything in It,* by Arthur Herman.

[52] See the June 19, 1972 Time Magazine article on the rise of Satanism in America; Anton Le Vey, the author of The Satanic Bible, founded "The Church of Satan" in 1966 in San Francisco. When membership in 1972 exceeded 10,000 he stopped keeping statistics. The website killuminatisoldiersoftruth.com identifies Marina Abramovic as the leading Satanic High Priestess in Hollywood; "She is the "spiritual advisor" and friend to many Hollywood stars and the power elite like Jay Z, Beyonce, Lady Gaga, Tom Petty, Chris Rock, Robert Deniro, Pam Anderson, Jared Leto, Johnny Depp, Gigi Hadid, James Franco, Bill Gates, Oprah, Bill and Hillary Clinton, Will Farrell, Elton John, Queen Beatrice, Kim Kardashian and many many more."

Christ is slipped in not in the fictional kingdom of Buttercup and Wesley, nor by the grandfather played by Peter Falk, but by the 10-year-old boy while he lay sick in bed. It is the one part in the otherwise excellent movie that is completely out of synch. What 10-year-old boy swears at his grandfather while he is reading him a book? Only a very bad one. But it seems to be the only way Reiner can take a stab at Jesus. That is the kind of son Hollywood promotes, not just in this movie but in hundreds of them. Normalizing blasphemy of Christ is critical to the rot of Western nations. It is frightening to know that during the rise of Hitler and The Third Reich, the Hollywood industry refused to criticize them during the 1930s. The excuse was that it did not want to hurt its sales in Germany. It may have also had something to do with the fact that much of Hollywood is Roman Catholic and from Germany, as was much of the German government at the time.

5. In Canada our latest Roman Catholic PM is doing all he can to break-up the alliance of the five primary nations which defeated Nazism, an alliance known as The Five Eyes. Repeatedly, he compromises their security interests and their requirements for military spending targets. At the same time, he does all he can to defend the influences of Communist China in Canada. It has now come to light that Canada has Chinese Government-controlled police stations operating all over the country, stations which the Liberal Party of Canada resists investigating. Which leads us to the next point.

6. One thing is clear, the Vatican has close ties with the Communist Government in China. Pope Francis has signed deals with that government which are so secretive that even RC leaders in China do not know what is in them, and in fact, the persecution of those leaders and their congregations has dramatically increased since their signing. Many RC leaders in China have either fled the country or gone into hiding since the pope's visits, and members of their congregations have been imprisoned for criticizing the Chinese Communist Party. Pope Frances has been silent about this persecution, and RCs in China say this "causes them confusion." Author Henry Sire, a Catholic historian, suggested Francis is playing a "geopolitical role as an enemy of the United States" in order to gain acclaim. The nefarious visits, where top secret Accords have been signed, were in September 2018, and renewed two years later. And, all were signed in the city of Wuhan!

7. The Vatican is in a struggle with the West, and particularly the

United States, according to Roman Catholic writers in the US.[53] This means signing agreements which strengthen China as an adversary of the United States have become of the utmost importance if any sort of rebalancing of power scales away from traditionally Protestant countries is to occur.

8. Distributism: When Rome says it is against the Communism of Russia, this does not mean that it is against the social construct of communism. It has repeatedly criticized what it terms the "injustice" of Capitalism. This is no surprise, since it was capitalism which dismantled the economic oppression of the era of The Holy Roman Empire over Western Europe. The principles of a socialist state completely align with its agenda, for at least two reasons:

   A. Socialist dictates allow Rome to distribute wealth from wealthier regions to poorer ones (with Rome taking the credit of "helping the poor." Poor Roman Catholic regions receive help from the largely Protestant nations during an emergency, not from the Vatican). During the Reformation, one of the main reasons for the willingness of northern European nations to listen to Protestant evangelists was the heavy Roman taxes they paid to support the Romanist enterprises (you know, those huge churches people go to visit?). This is the case even today in the EU; is it not true that those same northern kingdoms now subsidize the southern kingdoms, which are primarily under the grip of Catholicism?

   B. The second reason Rome favours socialism is that it destroys what is called the Middle Class. Before the Reformation, there

---

[53] An article in www.nationalinterest.org writes, "Zmirak, who is the author of "The Politically Incorrect Guide to Catholicism," said he worries Francis's Vatican is cultivating the China alliance as part of his struggle against the West, particularly the United States.

"Why else would the highest Vatican authority on economics, Bishop Marcelo Sorondo, take a carefully shepherded tour of China, then return claiming that this Communist dictatorship is the best practitioner of Catholic social teaching," Zmirak told the DCNF. The author, who is also the editor of conservative publication *The Stream*, was referring to remarks made by Sorondo following a 2018 visit to China.

"Right now, those who are best implementing the social doctrine of the Church are the Chinese," Sorondo told the Vatican Insider, applauding China's efforts to follow the green initiatives spelled out in Pope Francis' 2015 encyclical, Laudato Si. Sorondo also accused President Donald Trump of allowing himself to be manipulated by global oil firms and praised China for defending Paris Climate Accord."

was hardly a Middle Class. The Educated, Professional, and Businessman fared little better than the poor, as the book *The Protestant Ethic and the Spirit of Capitalism* proves so well. The trouble with an educated Middle Class is that they have time to think, plan, invent, study, and reflect on their situation and how to better themselves and the world around them. Galileo is one among many who found out how Rome treats those who think outside its box.

Nevertheless, Rome cannot come out and say that it is in favor of Communism and Socialism and Fascism because of the connections to Russia, Nazi Germany, and Italy/Spain/Bosnia. Where do these theories of wealth-distribution come from? Are they not simply the outgrowth of Vatican economic policy? I cite Wikipedia as evidence not because it is a solidly reliable source of information, but because it has a clear bent toward rewriting history in a way that protects Romanism. There are many websites like this now.

Distributism is an economic theory asserting that the world's productive assets should be widely owned rather than concentrated. Developed in the late 19th and early 20th centuries, distributism was based upon Catholic social teaching principles, especially Pope Leo XIII's teachings in his encyclical Rerum novarum (1891) and Pope Pius XI in Quadragesimo anno (1931).

Note when Romanism developed this theory: just before Communism and Socialism erupted on the world stage.

By taking apart democracies and their economies, and the freedoms which come along with constitutional republicanism and Capitalism are what had "developed in the late 19th and 20th centuries," they became the target of Rome's doctrine of Distributism. Rome no doubt plans on implementing its Distributism doctrine to dismantle them. It will do so out of "concern for the poor"—not to be included is the concentration of Rome's own vast gold reserves. Soon, if Rome gets its way, the world will be right back into the Dark Ages and under the grip of their own concentrated power and wealth.

9. When you think of the Ukraine war begun in 2022, consider this aspect; the Russian Orthodox Church is the last of the "Orthodox" church bodies which still refuses to acknowledge the Pope as the Universal Bishop. It has its own Patriarch, a position equivalent to the Pope. The Russians have not forgotten the support given by the Vatican to Hitler, even when he invaded Russia (with the additional support of soldiers from "neutral" RC countries like Spain and Portugal). As already noted, those involved in the creation of Russian Communism and the overthrow of the Tzar

were not only trained by RC priests in America, they also had an agreement to turn over that nation's gold to the Vatican, an agreement they broke when they saw how vast it was.

10. On 25 October 2020, a letter by *Archbishop Carlo Maria Viganò* ("the former Apostolic Nuncio to the United States of America") to President Trump, expressed the following: "Allow me to address you at this hour in which the fate of the whole world is being threatened by a global conspiracy against God and humanity." After identifying how the global elite intend to remake the world according to their liking through "The Great Reset," Vigano goes on to identify the key party responsible: The Pope. *"As is now clear, the one who occupies the Chair of Peter has betrayed his role from the very beginning in order to defend and promote the globalist ideology, supporting the agenda of the deep church, who chose him from its ranks."* If the leader of Roman Catholicism in the United States wrote an open letter to a sitting President of The United States saying, when read in full, that there is a coalition between the Global Elite and the Vatican to over throw the government of the United States, and install Joe Biden into the office of President as its "unscrupulous puppet" and that behind it is all is the "Enemy of the human race [the devil]", does that not call for an investigation into the Vatican itself?

Chapter Ten

President Trump Arrives

Few people thought that Donald J. Trump would run for the office of President of the United States. Only a short few years before he did, it seems even he did not think he would. What caused Trump to run for President is a matter of debate, and it likely was a combination of incidents. Having been a Democrat years before, and then a Republican, enabled Trump to see that the American political class cared little for the average American, or for the American systems which caused it to be such a success. America was run by the wealthy, and for the wealthy. As Trump famously said to Hilary Clinton in a debate, "The system is rigged for the wealthy." Clinton replied that it was not rigged. Trump, as a very wealthy man, replied, "Yes, it is rigged. I know, 'cause I use it." He said he did not put the system in place, rather she and her cronies did. Therefore, it is not illegal for him to use it. They made it legal!

This highlights one of the primary reasons much of the Political Establishment does not like Trump: he knows who they are, on both sides of the political divide in the US, and he does not approve of what they are doing to America. Like JFK, he is an America-first President.

Another reason they do not like him is because he cannot be bought. He does not need their money; he owes them no favors. He is the first president to be poorer after four years in office. Now, to be fair, remember that among America's wealthy, Donald Trump is well liked and respected by many. He golfs with them (he owns at least 18 elite golf courses), and he does business with them.

If you talk to people who have been long-term friends with Trump, or employees of his, it seems almost unanimous that he is well-liked and respected. He is "bombastic" and can be crude and blunt, but to characterize him in this way, and him alone among America's wealthy, would reveal an ignorance of reality or of its past Presidents. As a Canadian, I can attest that Trump would have a hard time getting elected in Canada. That is not the way we vote. On the other hand, in Canada, our greatest Prime Minister, Steven Harper, would have a hard time getting elected in the USA. Canada and the USA are very similar in many respects, and in others, very different, and our political situations are different. Canada is the only G7 country with only one nation on our border, and it is the most powerful nation in the history of the world, and we do not even guard the border with our military—yet we are a very wealthy nation! In the history of the world there is no country which has experienced the unique position of Canada.

We can afford to be "nice" and not get taken over as a result.

But the US has a very different situation, especially to their south. Canada could not be the country it is if it were in the geographical location of US. America must fight for its safety and security, and to run a country in their situation, they need a leader who is a fighter and an America-First President. If they don't have someone like that, they are in trouble.

Trump is that kind of President. It took time for the American people to realize it, but they desperately need someone like Trump. And the need for him seems to be growing since he left office. Why then is he so hated by some?

Like him or not, he is the most persecuted president in the history of the US. I propose that the hatred is a 4,000-year story, too. Now I will explain these two aspects, starting with that he is the most persecuted president in US history.

The Most Persecuted US President in History

From the moment Donald Trump said that he would run for the Presidency, saying that he was "attacked" would not be an overstatement. At first, he was ridiculed by the sitting president, Obama, as well as much of the media and talk shows. Then it got serious, and conspiracies came at him...that he was colluding with the Russians. The Clintons (it came out later) had paid for a document to be written and then leaked to the FBI and the media which claimed that it "linked" Trump to the Russian government.

Then the strangest thing of all occurred, something which has never happened in the history of the USA. All the living former presidents, both Republican and Democrat, campaigned *against* one of the two candidates. They were against Donald Trump becoming President. The Pope spoke strongly against him as well, something the Pontifex Maximus has never done before.

What was going on here? There is a very good explanation, and it is linked. Ever since Ronald Regan teamed up with the Pope to over-throw the USSR (and the media made this connection very clear), the US presidency has had a very close relationship with the Pope. It was Regan who started talking about a New World Order to come, too. All the presidents after Regan were part of secret student society from Yale University called *Skull and Crossbones*,[54] a secret society invented by the Roman Catholic secret

---

[54] It is hard to be certain about what secret societies Obama belongs to. Some say he is part of both the Illuminati and Skull and Bones, and some say just one of them. Obama is silent on the issue, though his top advisor, Austan Goolsbee was a Bonesmen. Groups of young Bonesmen were sometimes guests at the White House during Obama's time. It should be noted that in Germany the

society the Illuminati (many Bonesmen are part of the Illuminati).[55] The skull on the Bonesmen emblem is the same as the one on the Nazi officers' caps. Furthermore, all these Presidents, after they were elected, took a trip to the Vatican to kiss the Pope's ring, which is both an act of submission and of the Pope's approval for them to hold their office.[56]

This, it seems, is an echo of what the European kings had to do once they took office, otherwise the old Popes would say they have not received a divine rite to rule and should be overthrown.[57] This is what the ancient Babylonian priests bestowed on Julius Caesar in 63 B.C., who then turned the Roman Republic into the Roman Empire.

When Trump won the election, apparently it was customary for US presidents to visit three locations: Saudi Arabia, the Vatican, and the reigning monarch in Great Britain. The visit at Saudi Arabia seemed to go well for Trump. They seemed to respect him (they feel the opposite way about Biden). The Pope visit was very "awkward," especially after what he had said about Trump during the campaign. Trump was certainly in no mood to kiss the pope's ring, and did not hide the fact that the President of the United States had the endorsement of the People of the United States and the new President was satisfied with that. The Queen, who bowed to

---

Thule Society is a great deal like Skull and Bones. Adolf Hitler belonged to the Thule Society. One ritual, masturbating in an open coffin while singing satanic hymns with other members, is shared by both societies, and this act is thought by members to be a "born-again" experience (to Satan), a belief that was held by Hitler as well.

[55] The Illuminati have spewed many fiendish "frogs" out of its own putrid mouth, hasn't it? The Center for Foreign Relations (CFR), the Bilderberg Group, the Trilateral Group, the United Nations, Opus Dei which means "work of God," the Knights Templar, the Knights of Malta (with many non-Catholics as members), the Knights of Saint Columba founded in 1919, and the catholic Catenian association founded in 1908 in Manchester, as well as the well-known Priory of Sion, and the shadowy elusive Eleven, the Brotherhood of the Cross, and the dubious Club of Rome all added to this mix of magic and mysticism as well as the Masons and the Round Table Groups, and most were in the pockets of the Jesuits, yet not always aware of it.

[56] The funeral for Pope John Paul II was so important that the Bush Presidents and Clinton dropped what they were doing in order to go. All three together knelt before the dead man's body. Prince Charles delayed his wedding to go and kneel before the dead pope. Loyalty, or obligation and duty?

[57] One European king went against gaining the pope's approval to reign, and paid very dearly for it by having to perform several humiliating acts of submission before the pope would let him into the Vatican so that he could be installed on his throne.

the authority of the pope (though not nearly as much as Charles has since her death[58]), also knew that she was not America's monarch either. Trump walked in front of her, and never behind. The media made a big deal about it, but Trump sent the message anyway: America's President is servant to the American people alone.

The actual statement made by Trump's actions was this: in spite of the attempts of the Pope and his agents' efforts to gain control over America, and resurrect its ancient empire, Trump would have nothing to do with them or any of their secret societies. I do not think Trump had made all these connections, but as an America-first president as well as someone who was new to the inner world of politics, he wanted nothing to do with them.

---

[58] Note that 2010 pope Benedict gave to the Queen what he called "two pieces of the original cross of Jesus" to assist in the coronation of Charles. A ceremony in *the Coronation Church* then celebrated the occasion; it had been 1,000 years since a pope had entered there. After the pope shook hands with the Archbishop of the Church of England and the audience began to applaud. It was noted by some that, "Pope Benedict's wry smile betrayed his pleasure." In his speech of response, Benedict reminded them that the Mother Church was in Rome. This sounds far too much like the Dark Ages relationship between the Vatican and European monarchs of that time.

Chapter Eleven
Making America a Republic Again

Secondly, they hate Donald Trump because he was not shy about stating that no president got more done than he did. There is plenty of truth to this, and it may be just as true that there was no more that was needed for a president to do than when Trump was elected. Since the Regan era (1981-1987) America's debt has climbed to levels that cannot be truly appreciated, and its influence in the world has significantly declined. Their global policing role has increased, while their own infrastructure has declined to an embarrassing level. Trump, as an America-first President, was determined to switch that around.

It seemed that there was a coordinated effort by each successive administration toward this same end. On almost every level and from every angle America was weakened since Regan. Hilary Clinton, the wife of a President and Bonesmen, was scheduled by the Deep State machine —those who run the government of the USA who are not part of those who are elected—to become the President.

The mood in much of America was almost one of a resolve to observe its inevitable fall and demise. Hollywood produced movie after movie depicting America in tatters, whether it was a UFO invasion, Zombies, plague, War, some apocalypse was depicting the Statue of Liberty as suffering some terrible fate. The American people were being set up for a dim future. America was going the way great kingdoms went in the past, the talking heads repeated endlessly. "This was the way America must go too." This attitude groomed Western nations for decades that their end was nigh.

Then Trump arrived with the slogan, "Let's Make America Great Again." This was *the very last thing* the groups seeking to make America a Totalitarian State wanted to hear. Trump wanted America to be a Constitutional Republic again and sought to make the people of America believe in American freedom.

Once he was in office, the Deep State tried to do everything they could to cripple his administration. They tried to frame him with phony documents. They tried to impeach him, twice. The security agencies which were designed to protect the nation, were caught colluding to overthrow the elected President; they were spying on a presidential candidate on behalf of another candidate! Much of the media relentlessly criticized him. Even the PGA cancelled hosting the prestigious event at his Trump National Golf Club, Bedminster for the 2022 PGA Championship, a move which golfing legend Jack Nicklaus called the "cancel culture." This had been in place since 2014, and Trump had already spent millions of dollars in preparation for the event.

Why they relentlessly persecuted of Donald Trump is clear. He wants to rescue America from the planned demise of its Republic. Now the question is, *Who* is behind all this?

Upon compiling a list of those who have been in collusion to destroy the Trump presidency, it becomes clear that they are not a random collection of people from a variety of backgrounds. Rather, they are all connected; they have all kissed the Pope's ring. They either call themselves, "Good Catholics" or they have visited the Vatican to kiss his ring—the sign of submission to the authority he wields and to his program for the world.

Consider this partial list: Chuck Schumer, Nancy Pelosi, Mitch McConnell, Mike Pence, Anthony Fauci, Joe Biden, Gavin Newsom, most of the Supreme Court. They all call themselves "Good Catholics."

Then there are the people who, though not raised Roman Catholic, are both supportive of the pope's Great Reset agenda and have gone to the Vatican to both acknowledge the Pope's claim as Supreme Ruler—Pontifex Maximus—and to kiss his ring: Bill Gates, Barack Obama, Kamala Harris, George W Bush, George H.W. Bush, Bill Clinton, George Soros.

There could also be included in this list the vast majority of those who run the EU. I once started just checking of how many this is true of. I discovered that the clear majority of them all previously held positions within the Vatican's vast number of committees and organizations. This is also true at the UN, the Trilateral Commission, the World Bank (Klaus Schwab), the Davos Group, and more.

Upon examination, it should become clear that it is the Vatican who is coordinating The Great Reset and the New World Order. During the time leading up to World War 2, Rome had infiltrated many of the places of influence in the world, and we saw how Joseph Kennedy was a prime example. Even in England the wealthy Elite were "indifferent" to the threat posed by Nazism. This is why it was the East end of London which was bombed, and not the West end, where the rich lived. The rich most often are receptive of a Totalitarian type government which benefits the ultra-wealthy. Whereas a Constitutional Republic empowers the general population and argues for a justice system which applies as equally to the wealthy as to the poor.

A despotic aim

"But," the reader might say, "if they succeed at this, they will return the world into a dictatorship which would take away all the good Freedom has brought to the world? It would be a revival of what the Nazis were planning! All the developments that a Capitalistic economy has brought about, all its entrepreneurial spirit would be stifled—just like it was in communist Russia, which destroyed that entire society. We would be at the mercy of masters who could not be held accountable."

Yes, that is exactly what it would be like: absolute corruption. Surely what Lord Acton so aptly said about what too much power can do was true:

I cannot accept your canon that we are to judge Pope and King unlike other men, with a favourable presumption that they did no wrong. If there is any presumption it is the other way, against the holders of power, increasing as the power increases. Historic responsibility has to make up for the want of legal responsibility. Power tends to corrupt, and absolute power corrupts absolutely. Great men are almost always bad men, even when they exercise influence and not authority, still more when you super add the tendency or the certainty of corruption by authority. There is no worse heresy than that the office sanctifies the holder of it.

The generation which brought in the forms of Government now in place, like Lord Acton, were keenly aware of how their own generation had to fight for the freedom they sought to attain and preserve. Because it was during their time Western nations where freshly born, they were keenly aware of how very fragile their life was, and how badly their totalitarian enemies wanted to advance the overthrowing of free nations. Lord Acton and most of his contemporaries hated and deeply distrusted anything that smelled of Totalitarianism and repeatedly said so. Acton said many things like these quotes;

Despotic power is always accompanied by corruption of morality.

Authority that does not exist for Liberty is not authority but force.

Absolute power demoralizes.

Of the Roman Catholic writer Machiavelli, who wrote a book on how to manipulate the common people of the state in order to keep control of them, Lord Acton notes the heart of his problem with the book, *The Prince*:

The central idea of Machiavelli is that the state power is not bound by the moral law. The law is not above the state, but below it.

What Lord Acton was pointing out is that Machiavelli is offering advice on how to overthrow a constitutional republican style government, and how to keep a totalitarian state in place.[59] This was in line with his own Roman

---

[59] Lord Acton was raised a Roman Catholic, and like many of those observing world events in the 19th century (as already noted above), the totalitarianism of the Vatican was being exposed for what it was all over Europe, and the world.

Catholic beliefs about the position of the pope over governments.

Yes, this would indeed be awful. This is the very thing that was undone by the Protestant Reformation. When the Jesuits wrote *"It is better to rule a country ruined, than to rule a country heathen"*, they confirmed over 500 years ago that the Papacy *has been willing for centuries* to ruin any nation or all of them, when they seek to find a way out from under its control. The office of Supreme Pontiff believes that it has the right to ruin any nation or all of them rather than let that nation be free to rule itself.

When Vatican I began in 1869, it resulted in the dogma of Papal Infallibility which is surly the highest claim of any totalitarian state in the history of the world. This papal decision, as well as the ceasing of the publication *Home and Foreign Review*—of which Acton was the editor-- has long been acknowledged as decisive steps in Acton's progressive alienation from his fellow Catholics. Acton had been a loyal Roman Catholic, but became an outspoken critic of Catholic intolerance, suppression of individual thought, and especially Pope Pius IX notorious Syllabus of Errors (1864) especially as one of those "errors" called it "heresy" that "The Roman Pontiff can and ought to reconcile himself to, and agree with, progress, liberalism and recent civilization." It was Acton who in his most prophetic essay, "Nationality" (1862) which offered an early warning about the rise of totalitarianism, "Whenever a single definite object is made the supreme end of the State, be it the advantage of a class, the safety or the power of a country, the greatest happiness of the greatest number, or the support of any speculative idea, the State becomes for the time inevitably absolute. Liberty alone demands for its realization the limitation of the public authority, for liberty is the only object which benefits all alike, and provokes no sincere opposition."

Acton faulted Anglican priest Mandell Creighton, author of *History of the Papacy during the Period of the Reformation*, for not condemning the medieval Papacy — promoter of the Inquisition. But Acton and Creighton had a cordial correspondence which led to Acton's most unforgettable lines, written on April 5, 1887: "I cannot accept your canon that we are to judge Pope and King unlike other men, with a favourable presumption that they did no wrong. If there is any presumption it is the other way against holders of power, increasing as power increases. Historic responsibility has to make up for the want of legal responsibility. Power tends to corrupt and absolute power corrupts absolutely."

Late in his life, when he was a lecturer at Cambridge, Acton stated, that "States based on the unity of a single race, like modern Italy and Germany, would prove a danger to liberty." That statement, made around the turn of the 20th century, turned out to be prophetic of the two world wars soon to come.

Acton, it seems, came to discover that he was born into the very system which he turned against: Totalitarianism.

If my reader is still in doubt that now, at the beginning of 2024, things are finally different, and that the Pontifex Maximus in Rome has no such intentions as world domination, then I have only one more point.

As the presidency of Donald Trump was ending, at the end of 2020, he received several open letters by none other than the highest-ranking Roman Catholic in the United States. Archbishop Carlo Maria Viganò wrote to then President Donald Trump of a conspiracy at the Vatican to overthrow the government of the United States and install their puppet, Joe Biden. It is titled *Letter #32, Friday, October 30, 2020: Vigano to Trump.* Below are selected excerpts from it:

Mr. President,

Allow me to address you at this hour in which the fate of the whole world is being threatened by a global conspiracy against God and humanity.

I write to you as an Archbishop, as a Successor of the Apostles, as the former Apostolic Nuncio to the United States of America...

A global plan called the Great Reset is underway.

Its architect is a global élite that wants to subdue all of humanity, imposing coercive measures with which to drastically limit individual freedoms and those of entire populations.

In several nations this plan has already been approved and financed; in others it is still in an early stage.

Behind the world leaders who are the accomplices and executors of this infernal project, there are unscrupulous characters who finance the World Economic Forum and Event 201, promoting their agenda.

The purpose of the Great Reset is the imposition of a health dictatorship aiming at the imposition of liberticidal measures, hidden behind tempting promises of ensuring a universal income and cancelling individual debt...

In the religious sphere, this obstacle to evil is the Church, and in particular the papacy; in the political sphere, it is those who impede the establishment of the New World Order.

As is now clear, the one who occupies the Chair of Peter has betrayed his role from the very beginning in order to defend and promote the globalist ideology, supporting the agenda of the deep church, who chose him from its ranks...

Around you are gathered with faith and courage those who consider you the final garrison against the world dictatorship.

The alternative is to vote for a person who is manipulated by the deep state, gravely compromised by scandals and corruption, who will do to the United States what Jorge Mario Bergoglio [Pope Francis] is doing to the Church, Prime Minister Conte to Italy, President Macron to France, Prime Minster Sanchez to Spain, and so on.

The blackmailable nature of Joe Biden – just like that of the prelates of the Vatican's "magic circle" – will expose him to be used unscrupulously, allowing illegitimate powers to interfere in both domestic politics as well as international balances.

Vigano is surely a brave man for standing up to the Vatican, and to Pope Francis. Millions have died a torturous death for far, far less. However, Vigano is sadly naive to think that this all started on 13 March 2013 when Jorge Mario Bergoglio was elected Pope. There has been a long history of Vatican vulgarity and slander against the Republic of the United States, Constitutional Republicanism, Capitalism, freedom of conscience, and especially Protestantism of the Reformed/Presbyterian type (the original protestants). It is them which built Western government systems. Isn't it obvious, therefore, where, and why the "Cancel Culture" -- promoted in the five countries who defeated their attempt at a Third Reich of a thousand year--is coming from? The culture, history, laws, economy, freedoms, and government systems of these nations are distinctly not Roman Catholic and anti-totalitarian. They were intentionally set up by those who fled these things in Europe to keep it from infiltrating them. That is why they must be "cancelled" … no matter what it takes. For Vigano to understand this, he would have to abandon much of what he has promoted for his whole life and adopt what its Protestant opponents have erected—what Christ Jesus has erected—over the last 500 years.

If this kind of letter, from the man with the most senior rank within Catholicism in America, is not enough to open the eyes of a thinking person, then there is nothing more that can be said. The letter in full clearly links The Great Reset to powerful individuals cooperating with the Supreme Roman Pontiff.

Allow me to now assess where all this might be going.

Chapter Twelve

A New World Order (Again)

My goal now is to briefly suggest what is likely coming due to the world-wide effort to establish the Supreme Pontiff to absolute power. He, inspired by the spirit behind him, has sought to regain this throne, lost since the Tower of Babel was destroyed by God.

Just about every Christian Missionary agency in the world is reporting the same thing right now; the Christian Church is growing around the world, and there is hardly any country left where it is not growing. In many places it is growing so fast it is hard to keep track of it. Some friends of mine were telling me that during summer about ten years-ago they went to a remote country in central Asia (having no known Christian presence) to plant a church. By God's grace, they planted a small church. Then the group of pastors had to return to North America. They wanted to return the following summer, but could not. The second summer they were able to return and were just hoping that the church was still functioning. What they found instead was a thriving church, which had planted 10 more churches, and the original congregation had no idea how many churches those ten churches were in the process of planting. "Bring us Bibles," they said to the pastors when they left. "Bring us materials to help us teach the people," was all they asked for.

All over the world this kind of growth is happening, though you rarely hear about it.

At the same time however, Roman Catholicism's congregations are being devastated. In Canada they shut one of their buildings, so I am told by the local RC diocese, every week. This is a complicated process, logistically, due to municipal regulations. They have teams of people whose responsibility it is to make this happen in accordance with by-laws. The diocese also told me that in some provinces in Canada, there is not even one parish who has a priest serving it who is from Canada. They are *all* either from Nigeria or the Philippines. Most of them cannot be understood when they try to speak English. This, of course, is only increasing the lapse in attendance by those raised Roman Catholic.

This exodus from Romanism is going on around the world (Revelation 18:4). African nations which were once stanchly Roman Catholic are seeing serious declines. The Rwandan Genocide in 1994, it soon became clear, was significantly influenced by the RC priests.[60] It was they who also offered their buildings as safe places to hide, only for the hapless victims to brutally discover that the murdering bands were in league with the priests. It was also discovered that some of the priests had demonized the Tutsi to the Hutus in their congregations, saying that they "were not real humans." The language they used often sounded like what the priests told their congregations in France about the Jews leading up to the Nazi invasion.

It is stories like these which spread around Africa, and caused the dramatic decline in attendance. The Congo is likely the most violent and poverty-stricken country on earth. Yet, it is also the most Roman Catholic country in Africa. These things do not go unnoticed by the African people anymore. The people of the Congo are starting to make the connection too.

South America, once a bastion for Roman Catholicism, has seen a serious decline of attendance at The Mass and a significant increase in attendance at Protestant churches over the last 40-50 years.

Spain was once the most loyal Roman Catholic country in Europe. While Francisco Franco was President, Roman Catholicism was strictly and cruelly enforced by this military general through his Nationalist forces. When he overthrew the Second Spanish Republic (note; *Republic*), his goal was to create a thoroughly Roman Catholic state. From 1939 to 1975, this dictator ruthlessly used his police force to torture and even kill anyone in the country who was not Roman Catholic enough—it was said that Franco was more Catholic than the Pope. Note when he came to office; 1939—the beginning of WW2.

I have read reports by Christian missionaries working among the Spanish people. They report that all have someone in their family who was either tortured and/or killed under Franco, or, someone in their family were one of those who participated in the torture and/or murdering. Missionaries from South America who speak Spanish report that they have a very hard time sharing the Good News about Jesus due to the lingering hostility toward Roman Catholicism—the only expression of Christianity they know. The mission agency reports that the Spanish people are not merely indifferent when hearing about Christianity, they are angry—even hostile to the Bible itself, or its message—to anything that reminds them of

---

[60] These priests, I have read, were moved to Rwanda when the Quiet Revolution in Quebec, Canada, devastated attendance there. Attendance went from 98% of the population, to 2% within about a decade—a complete reversal. This resulted in many "excess" priests, who were then moved to Rwanda. This is a common practice, to which the priests—who almost always have only one skill: saying the Mass—are obligated to accept if they want employment.

Romanism. Many have never even heard of Protestantism, and must be re-educated about the Bible's message, so different from the twisted one they were indoctrinated into.

In 2021, a report found that about 3,000 persons working for the Vatican, most of whom are priests, had assaulted more than 330,000 children over the previous 70 years in France. Suspicions are that the number is much higher, but many victims do not want to come forward and thereby reawaken their traumatic ordeals as the hands of those who are part of the Vatican system. Reports say that the Protestant churches are growing tremendously in the country.

I have only given a few instances about the state of the religious side of Romanism as far as attendance at Mass. The story is the same all around the world. Rome claims to have 1.3 billion adherents, but the actual number is only a small fraction of that (for example, it is likely that since I was baptized RC, I am still included in that number).

Given the amount of societal moral corruption that is coming to light from within Roman Catholicism, sexually, in banking, in espionage, and in a departure of even maintaining a facade of adhering to the Bible's teachings, many historic Mass attendees are rebelling. One American Roman Catholic website suggested that over 50% of US congregations would be supportive of separating themselves from Rome and forming a new "denomination".

There are too many incidents raised to explain why those raised Roman Catholic are feeling betrayed by the Vatican, but maybe two very modern ones would suffice. In 2018, Pope Francis commemorated the implementation of a huge statue of the pagan god Moloch at the entrance to the Colosseum in Rome. The history of child sacrifice which Moloch infamously required of his worshippers mattered not to the Pontiff. With its role in the implementation of abortion in many countries, few are surprised.

If this were not enough, on March 5, 2021, immediately after the Biden inauguration to the White House (where the Pope was invited to give a speech to Congress, outlining the evils of Capitalism), the Vatican arranged for a meeting at the Ziggurat[61] in Ur, Iraq—the same one which would have

---

[61] On Rome's use of a Ziggurat as a symbol of its world religion, consider how the 1988 version of the NIV structures Revelation 17:5, which speaks of "the great prostitute" and how it resembles a Ziggurat;
"This title was written on her forehead;
MYSTERY
BABYLON THE GREAT
THE MOTHER OF PROSTITUTES
AND OF THE ABOMINATIONS OF THE EARTH"

been there during Abraham's time. Romanism had been rebuilding it since 1999 in anticipation of this very event—for the gathering of leaders of the world's various religions. There, the Pontiff led them in a call of cooperation as an interfaith body to solve the world's problems as a world-wide pluralistic religious body. This, he said, was what God called them to do in his message to Abraham so long ago. God, he told them, promised Abraham that he would be the Father of Pluralism in Ur, "the birthplace of all religions," a prophesy which was only now being fulfilled on that day.

Dear brothers and sisters,

This blessed place brings us back to our origins, to the sources of God's work, to the birth of our religions.

Here, where Abraham our father lived, we seem to have returned home. It was here that Abraham heard God's call; it was from here that he set out on a journey that would change history.

We are the fruits of that call and that journey. God asked Abraham to raise his eyes to heaven and to count its stars.

In those stars, he saw the promise of his descendants; he saw us.

Today we, Jews, Christians, and Muslims, together with our brothers and sisters of other religions, honour our father Abraham by doing as he did: we look up to heaven and we journey on earth. Thousands of years later, as we look up to the same sky, those same stars appear. They illumine the darkest nights because they shine together.

Heaven thus imparts a message of unity: the Almighty above invites us never to separate ourselves from our neighbours.

This is the Pontifex Maximus, the grand "Bridge-Builder" between all the world's religions, seeking to bring them together as one body. And note carefully that the pope tells them that the Ziggurat there in ancient Babylonia, is "the birthplace of *their* religions." The only religion whose birthplace is in Babylon, is The Tower of Babel religion.

But even someone with a superficial understanding of the story of Abraham as found in Genesis knows that God was not calling Abraham *into* Pluralism, but rather *out* of it. The Ziggurat in Ur, modeled on the Tower of

---

One must ask if the symbol of a Ziggurat, so commonly known by the Early Church who lived in the region of the Middle East, was not a message that John was sending to the seven churches; that the enemy of God is the resurrection and preservation of ancient Babylonian religion in the City on Seven Hills: Rome, the very city which the next verse goes on to describe as, "the woman was drunk with the blood of the saints." (Rev.17:6) No one has been responsible for the murder of more Christians than Rome.

Babel—the very place from which all pagan religions and pagan governments arose from—the pope used as a beacon to call all religions back into unity as they were at the Tower's founding. This is the very opposite of God's call to Abraham.

However, the truth is, God was calling Abraham to leave the pluralism represented by that Ziggurat in Ur almost 4,000 years ago, and to worship Him alone through Christ Jesus, the true "bridge-builder" between God and Mankind. He is the one through whom "ascending and descending" is possible between God and Man (Genesis 28:12 with John 1:51).

Joshua not only explains to the Hebrews the need to leave such pluralism, like Abraham, as they left Egypt (including Egypt's pluralism, which also came out of Babylon), but he references in his speech for the Hebrews to what Abraham did;

Joshua said to all the people, "This is what the LORD, the God of Israel, says: 'Long ago your forefathers, including Terah the father of Abraham and Nahor, lived beyond the River and worshiped other gods. But I took your father Abraham from the land beyond the River and led him throughout Canaan and gave him many descendants...

Now fear the LORD and serve him with all faithfulness. Throw away the gods your forefathers worshiped beyond the River and in Egypt, and serve the LORD. (Joshua 24:2-4; 14)

You see, the Pontiff is building a religion, and is using Abraham as a model. But what he is actually attempting is to rebuild the religious Pluralism which characterized both of the 1,000-year reigns of the Roman Empire, and that of the Holy Roman Empire which had a policy of "meeting the pagans half-way." He is trying to undo what God did when he divided the peoples at The Tower of Babel, by building a bridge between them through himself.

These actions, an outright rejection of anything remotely related to Biblical teaching, and the embrace of the very opposite, are what are causing many of those raised Roman Catholic in America, and in the world, to see through to the real religion behind the Vatican's veil. It was always there, make no mistake, from the beginning, back to its 4,000-year-old origins. In the past the veil was thicker; the "Christian veneer" of the real Vatican was more pronounced. But as Romanism becomes more desperate, its true-self is now almost impossible to hide.[62]

---

[62] Alexander Hislop anticipated that it would be an event like this which would finally reveal the true identity of the Pontifex Maximus; "In the Apocalyptic visions it is just before the judgment upon her that, for the first time, John sees

the Apostate Church with the name Babylon the Great 'written upon her forehead' (Rev. 17:5).

What means the writing of that name 'on the forehead'? Does it not naturally indicate that, just before judgment overtakes her, her real character was to be so thoroughly developed, that everyone who has eyes to see, who has the least spiritual discernment, would be compelled, as it were, on ocular demonstration, to recognize the wonderful fitness of the title which the Spirit of God had affixed to her? Her judgment is now evidently hastening on and just as it approaches, the Providence of God, conspiring with the Word of God, by light pouring in from all quarters, makes it more and more evident that Rome is in very deed the Babylon of the Apocalypse, that the essential character of her system, the grand objects of her worship, her festivals, her doctrine and discipline, her rites and ceremonies, her priesthood and their orders, have all been derived from ancient Babylon, and finally, that the Pope himself is truly and properly the lineal representative of Belshazzar.

In the warfare that has been waged against the domineering pretensions of Rome it has too often been counted enough merely to meet and set aside her presumptuous boast that she is the mother and mistress of all churches—the one Catholic Church, out of whose pale there is no salvation. If ever there was excuse for such a mode of dealing with her, that excuse will hold no longer. If the position I have laid down can be maintained, she must be stripped of the name of a Christian Church altogether, for if it was a Church of Christ that was convened on that night when the pontiff-king of Babylon, in the midst of his thousand lords, 'praised the gods of gold and of silver and of wood and of stone' (Dan. 5:4), then the Church of Rome is entitled to the name of a Christian Church, but not otherwise. This to some, no doubt, will appear a very startling position, but it is one which it is the object of this work to establish, and let the reader judge for himself whether I do not bring ample evidence to substantiate my position." (Introduction)

Chapter Thirteen

The Break Up of the EU Empire?

Another very serious blow to the Vatican's Great Reset agenda is the almost complete breakup of the EU. Great Britain's exit was a serious blow, to be sure. It cost the EU the loss of significant revenue, and it opened the door for others to leave more easily. But the cracks of *all* the major countries wanting to leave is becoming very hard to hide. France is burning with riots, and while the media wants us to believe it has to do with merely pension reform, the truth is that the French people want to leave the EU, they want to avoid being drawn into a NATO war with Russia, and they want the banking stooge Emanuel Macron taken out of office. Italy's new Prime Minister, Georgia Maloni, is openly rebelling against the EU, their migrant-immigration policy, and the looming war against Russia – which has caused prices in the country to make life for the average person to become unbearable. Even Germans are wanting a referendum on leaving the EU, and their complaints are like that of France and Italy. Holland, the second largest food exporter in the world, is in open rebellion to the EU. The EU plan to confiscate land from their farmers has given rise to the BBB party, which has as its primary purpose a policy of opposing the EU, especially when it comes to their policy toward land ownership. It is so serious that in 5 years they went from just beginning as a party, to being the most powerful party in the country. Poland is resisting the EU on almost every level and refuses to accept their Muslim immigration agenda as well. They too are proposing to have a Referendum.

Let the reader note that, relatively speaking, it was not all that long ago that the kings, the ultra-wealthy and the Vatican especially owned practically all the farmland in Europe. At that time farmers were but Serfs, farming the land for the rich, and barely getting by. That land was confiscated in the 19th century, and given to the people. What we are seeing in Europe is a grand effort to get that land back again. As the New Year turned in 2024, there are wide-spread demonstrations all over Europe about how their governments are attempting to take that land back again. The excuse is environmental, as was planned at the first Club of Rome meeting in 1968. But dominance is the more likely goal, as Capitalism and private ownership of property is mostly incompatible with both European monarchies, and the Vatican.

So, with these nations in open revolt against the EU, the ones which surely make up the heart of the EU now that Great Britain has left, there is an obvious question: **What or Who is holding it together?** The answer cannot be merely political, and it is certainly not economical since these five leading nations support most of the other weaker nations in the Union. The answer must be religious. The leading religion in Europe has its headquarters in Rome. Rome has been the leading city of Western Europe for the last 2400 years since the conquering of Carthage and their general, Hannibal. Even more so, its Pontiff claims to be king of all three levels of existence; Heaven, Earth and Under the earth. Surely Western Europe is seen by him as simply an entitlement, the least of the world that is his, until he gets all of it. Romanism claims that no nation's leader can legitimately be in office without his approval. Worse yet, he claims to be The Head of the Church; even Jesus Christ's representative. And some of the popes have *claimed* to be God. Such a person, such a seat, needs a kingdom, and the Pontiff of Rome has always laid first claim on Western Europe over all other challengers.

Therefore, what other explanation can there be to what is holding the European Union together than the Vatican, over which the flag of its Mother Mary, Queen of the Universe, Queen of Heaven[63] flies? In the city of Montreal, Canada, in the building named, *Mary; Queen of Heaven* people are called to worship at the Mass. In his article, *Babylon and Rome*, Dr. F.F. Bruce carefully traces "Catholic ritual" back, not to the New Testament, but to Babylon.[64] The link between the EU, Romanism and Babylon, cannot be seriously denied.

What does this mean for the future? It means that the Vatican is getting very desperate. They narrowly failed in WW1 and then again in WW2, and the Vatican was nearly bankrupt when WW2 was over. Now, trying for a third time, history shows they will stop at nothing.

The UN has become a weapon as well. Its original purpose was to create a place where nations could work out their differences, with the goal was avoiding another World War. What it has become is something very different. Robert Malone speaks of how it has morphed into a pseudo-world government with an agenda to rule the world.

There's a bill in the United Nations right now asserting that, in the case of a public health emergency, a new constitution that the UN would create would circumvent – be placed over – all of the Western Democracy constitutions.[65]

---

[63] This is the very title of given to Nimrod's mother/consort in Ezekiel 44:17, the worship of which had enslaved the Jews into open rebellion toward God – causing God to destroy the Temple.

[64] *Babylon and Rome*, F.F. Bruce, *The Evangelical Quarterly* 13: p.241-261.

[65] Dr. Robert Malone, author of, *The UN Security Council in the 21st Century*, in an article titled: *Time to Flush Out All WEF Members from Our Governments* (May 14, 2022; The Golden Age of Gaia).

It does not take long to figure out that they are all in league with each other. They have set a date to accomplish their One World Government and one Religion of Pluralism: 2030. How is it that the United Nation, The World Economic Forum, The Vatican, etc. etc., all have the same date for the Great Reset, if they are not all working together?

And why that date? Because it is very religious. It is the date which corresponds to the crucifixion of Jesus. The Bible tells us that Jesus predicted that the Temple would be destroyed "one generation" after the crucifixion (Matthew 24:2, 34). The Temple was destroyed in 70 A.D., meaning that Jesus most likely said these words in 30 AD. At least, the timing works for those who are looking for a way to "celebrate" a New World Order by giving the world a Great Reset and, in the Vatican's mind, returning the world to a pre-Reformation condition politically, economically and in restricting freedoms (It is interesting, remember, that Romanism, Islam and Judaism all consider the years 1300-1500 as their Golden Era.)

All this must be in place before the 2030 date, and for this purpose they have created such an organization. We can also expect the World Health Organization (WHO) to be used more and more to dismantle the sovereignty of the world's constitutional republics. In the Spring of 2024, the WHO has requested that the 194 member states vote to give them the authority to supersede the constitutions of any nation as they see fit, so long as they deem it for the good of the world's health. Beyond this, they seek to create a New Pandemic Treaty to give them powers beyond individual nations. We are not surprised that it is individual nation's constitutions which are being targeted. Take away a nation's ability to appeal to its own constitution by an authority outside of that nation, and you will have rendered it no longer a republic. You will have transformed it from republic to empire, just as Julius Caesar did to Rome. The elected Senate will be an authority in name only, subject to the will of their unelected and unaccountable totalitarian emperor system.

Chapter Fourteen
Old Allies Resurrected

We can expect illegal immigration from the Roman Catholic countries to the south of America under the Joe Biden Administration, and with the aid of the Roman Catholic buildings along the path of their journey, to continue.

We can also expect the rise of Rome's old allies. The treaties signed between Rome and Islam secures illegal immigration into all of Europe, and all over the world.

Canada saw a significant rise in illegal immigrants from Haiti via the border with the State of New York under the Roman Catholic PM, Justin Trudeau. As well, unprecedented numbers of people have immigrated into Canada after the Media slandered PM Steven Harper out of office, and shoe-horned Trudeau into it. Canada has a serious housing problem as a result, but the Liberal Party only talks of *increasing* immigration, quickly. Time is running short.

This is coupled with the resurrection of the old monarchies all over Europe. I was surprised to read about how involved these historic totalitarian rulers of Europe, supposedly divinely appointed to their thrones, were involved in The Great Reset.

An Asian ally, like Japan was in WW2, has already been secured in China. This was already discussed above.

Reading world history demonstrates that society has changed a great deal after 1920. Things we take for granted today, as part of regular life, are very recent developments. Before this decade (1920-30) there was, for example, a very large gap between the average laborer's income and that of the large business owner. The position of the large business owner was dramatically strengthened over his employees by the support of the government who used the police force to keep the disparity in place.

Here in Canada, however, veterans of WW1 forced a change. Arriving home after four years of war, since many of them had left when they were still in their teens, they were now battle-hardened young men looking to make a future in the land they fought and died to see set free. They came back to cronyism. They first had to fight the government to fairly compensate them for four years of hell in the trenches of Europe. Then, as they sought employment, the pay they were offered was an insult.

"Demonstrations and Protests" broke out in the city of Winnipeg. The usual way of dealing with them (calling in the police) was used. But what the police discovered was that these veterans had been dealing with a far worse enemy for the previous four years, and that the veterans among the protesters could respond with a level of violence that the police had never seen before. So, foolishly, the police were told by the government to increase the pressure. A few demonstrators were even shot, right here in Canada.

The foolishness of this action was soon realized when the veterans among the demonstrators made it clear that they had just witnessed the worst butchery Europe had ever seen, so they were not at all intimidated. Policemen were pulled off of their horses and beaten. But the real target became the politicians who had given the orders. Fliers were distributed advertising these targets. In swift response, the government established significant adjustments to wages and workers benefits, and heads cooled.

The end of WWI also resulted in The Lord's Day Act. This meant that in Canada businesses had to be closed on Sunday. Workers had to get one day off, and that so that they could go to church with their families. This produced what we now call, Weekends; Saturdays became optional work-days. Being closed on The Lord's Day (Sunday), stopping the factories once a week, made it a whole lot easier to close them for two days.

This cost employers money, and for the government, created a whole new Middle Class, and there soon grew to be many in this class. The extra money freed up leisure-time. Instead of living practically hand-to-mouth, almost everyone had time to think about their country and how it was run. And worse, for the government and big business, that meant the little guys would get involved.

This movement was the beginning of unions. Not like they are now, but as they were originally intended: to protect the little guy from the elite. What happened in Canada was happening all over the Western world. It was the rise of a republican state against a totalitarian state atmosphere. Not that the Canadian government was totalitarian, because it was not. However as demonstrated throughout the course of this paper, the vestiges of Totalitarianism began to dismantle in the 16th century. The 17th and 18th centuries were full of the dismantling of totalitarian powers, as we have already seen. In the 19th century there was a renewed push to remove still more of how the world used to be. Our discussion about Lord Acton was typical of great thinkers and actors in those times. Then, in the 1920s they took it to a new level.

As the 20th century emerged, the World Wars brought about an even greater distrust of those who sought too much power. Books like *Animal Farm* by George Orwell (1945) made many school children aware of the dangers of those who believe that "All animals are all equal, but some animals are more equal than others." (p.103) He followed this up with *1984* (1949), further warning about the rising dangers of "Big Brother" as a form of justification by governments "caring" for us, with the end goal being the establishment of totalitarianism.

He was so right. Here lies the great present danger: *1984* is not read in the schools anymore, and most people in the Western world do not realize that what we have right now is an incredible anomaly in history. There has never been a time of prosperity for the average person in all of history, in any nation throughout all of time, like what we experience in North America right now (the Pope, of all people, calls this Greed!). Indeed, the whole world is better off now than they have ever been. It was not until 1925 that the Americans and the British finally stamped out the sale of human beings, slavery. It cost them a great deal of money, mainly fighting the countries around the Mediterranean Sea. It cost them the lives of their sailors, to finally stop the Islamists who were stealing human beings from the coasts of Europe (called White Slavery) and the coasts of Africa (African Slavery) to sell them.

What is The Great Reset but an effort to return the Elite, the Super-Rich, the Monarchies, and Rome to their positions of unquestionable dominance over the vast majority of people? Like the Ziggurat on the back of the US One Dollar bill. Over the last 40 years or so, through national debts, there has been a gargantuan transfer of wealth to those behind The Great Reset. We are now at the point where 80% of the world's wealth is in the hands of .01% of the world's population. COVID only made this far, far worse. There is a huge problem with the centralization of powers, and always has been, but we are seeing this being advanced. Whether it is Digital Identification, government controlled digital currency, health controlled by the World Health Organization (WHO), or the United Nations seeking to have authority over national governments, the plan to centralize power is being foisted upon the world. As I write the farms of many European Union countries are threatened by their governments for confiscation. This is but the restoration of the control the Vatican had, through its kings, back before the 19th century when their huge tracts of land were taken away from her.

This much is sure: The Great Reset, planned by the world's elite, will ruin life for the average person (expect even "weekends" to disappear). It was freedom from them that created the wealth we enjoy. Not them. They did what they could to try and stop it.

There will be a continued weakening of the traditional family, too. Why? The nuclear family is essential to stability. Stability threatens totalitarianism, because instability weakens people. So, lobbies such as the LGBTQ will continue to push. I am told by someone in that community that soon "MAP" is their next addition to their acronym; Minor Attracted

Persons. Expect that the effort will continue to be desensitize your children to anything like Christian morality (the morality which most Westerners now simply assume, without knowing where it comes from). At a homosexual rally in the US some of the participants were chanting, "We're here. We're queer, we're coming for your children." Expect pornography and other temptations designed to turn children away from marital faithfulness to become increasingly more mainstream. The Pope himself, in support of this agenda, happily uses people's chosen pronouns and "blesses" same-sex unions.

Few people have taken the time to become aware of what life was like before the Protestant Reformation took place. Western Europe was immoral, poor, uneducated, and demoralized. And in no place on earth was there more immorality than in the city of Rome. When Martin Luther took his first trip there from Germany in the early 16th century, he was overwhelmed by the corruption. The closer he got to the Vatican and its priests, the worse it got. The Pope at the time, Leo X, received for his birthday a giant cake. The top opened, and out jumped naked little boys; his birthday presents. Luther eventually wrote a book titled, *The Babylonian Captivity of the Church.*

That is the world they are trying to reset to. A documentary recently came out about how much child sex trafficking there is in the world: *The Sound of Freedom.* My son told me he only got an hour into watching it, and had to turn it off. This is a serious problem around the world. The president of Russia, Vladimir Putin, in his 2016 New Year's address to the nation talked about the need for Russia to return to its Christian foundations, especially in morality. Whether this was politicking or not, I will leave that to my readers to decide (how that would be politicking when most of the nation does not attend a church is bewildering). What he went on to say is revealing. Putin said that Russia should realize that the world is being run by a small group of sexually deviant people, many of whom are part of international child sex rings. Maybe this is related to NATO's support of the war in Ukraine?

We should expect to see the push of sexual deviancy used to erode the Christian norms our countries, without which they will collapse.[66] Immorality and crime are a great drain on a county's self-worth and finances.

Finally, The End:

Why is the system which is Rome so hard to defeat? I will offer two reasons.

---

[66] Outlining just how depraved the plan is for Western nations is a talk given by Laura Aboli called *Transhumanism: The End Game.*

People generally gravitate toward a government that reflects their religion and their morality. With rejection of the God of the Bible, and the Bible as His Word to us, even His *Constitution* to us, comes a rulership without God at the top. When that develops, there are only two rulership options left to fill the gap. The first is what Romanism represents: a man who thinks he is above all other men - that he is a law unto himself - that he is God. That is historic Totalitarianism—that is what Romanism came to champion, beginning with Julius Caesar when he took on the title of Pontifex Maximus from the exiled priests of Babylon. In Thessalonians 2:3 the Bible predicted a man who would come who would believe that he is a law unto himself, a man who thinks even God's law doesn't apply to him; a "lawless one." [67]

Don't let anyone deceive you in any way, for that day will not come until the rebellion occurs and the man of lawlessness is revealed, the man doomed to destruction.

The philosophy of government which rose from the Tower of Babel, originated in the Garden of Eden. When the serpent spoke to Eve, and to her husband as he silently submitted and forfeited his role as Garden Keeper—the role assigned to him before the woman was created (Genesis 2:15-18) that they could be like God, and be submissive to no one. When he abandoned that role, the serpent promised that they would be gods. But it was the serpent who ended up being their master (Ephesians 2:1-3). It was all a lie. That is what happens when we do not obey God's law. We get a tyrant over us.

"You will not surely die," the serpent said to the woman, "For God knows that in the day that you eat of it you will be like God, knowing good and evil. When the woman saw that the fruit of the tree was good for food and desirable for gaining wisdom, she took some and ate it. She also gave some to her husband who was with her, and he ate of it also."

The second reason is that Rome is the inheritor of the spiritual force behind the Tower of Babel; the voice to Adam and the Woman in the Garden. There is a real demonic world. And there are spirits behind the forces which seek to rule the world. You may not believe that, and many of those they influence do not believe it, but that does not make them go away.

---

[67] Professor Smith writes regarding the ancient position of Pontiff, "The pontiffs themselves were not subject to any court of law or punishment, and were not responsible either to the senate or to the people." The pontiff was subject to no law whatsoever. For further information about the ancient role of the Pontifex Maximus, see
https://www.perseus.tufts.edu/hopper/text?doc=Perseus:text:1999.04.0063:entry=pontifex-cn

The book of Daniel, in the Bible, briefly introduces us to the reality of this world (chapters 10 and 11). Rome is the home of the most powerful of those forces, brought to them by the exiled priests of Babylon.

What the Apostle Paul told the church in Ephesus is generally true of the world, and surely most true about Rome; *For our struggle is not against flesh and blood, but against the rulers, against the authorities, against the powers of this dark world and against the spiritual forces of evil in the heavenly realms.* (Ephesians 6:12).

When Mother Theresa decided to live out her last days praying in the Vatican, she thought she was going to live in peace. Instead, she was so overcome by the spiritual forces there, she had to have herself exorcised of demons, three times. Such is the power behind what is in the New Babylon. Such is why it is so hard to defeat.

Do you remember the part in the *Lord of the Rings* Trilogy, the last movie in the series, when the enemies of the White City are defeated, and the main characters are sitting in the castle enjoying the victory? The temptation during times of prosperity is to sit back and enjoy the rest the battle achieved. Gimli says to his companions in reference to Sauron now defeated and penned up in his home base, "Let him rot in there." Aragorn knew better. He knew his fathers, the kings of old, were slowly seduced as time went by. He knew that if Frodo and Sam were not able to deliver the final blow, history would only repeat itself again and again. That is why Aragorn insisted that they not be satisfied with a temporary peace. They had to see the Ring destroyed.

After WW2 the Allied powers were tired of war, tired of people dying. They, like Gimli, either thought the Roman Pontiff had learned his lesson, or that he would just "rot in his castle." As has happened so many times in history, Rome was allowed to rebuild. That is why Rome is so hard to defeat. We do not have the power to finally defeat her—but God does.

Chapter Fifteen

God Comes to Us

In the introduction it was noted that many believe, "our modern crisis is not economic, political, scientific or technological, and that 'no answers' will be found in those spheres. I believe that we are living through a deep spiritual crisis; perhaps even a spiritual war." We suggested that this is truer than many may want to realize. Now you see what was meant by that. The battle is now very serious, and for the Tower Religion, it cannot lose this time. It has shown its hand, and there is no putting the veneer back in place.

If you want to know what is ultimately coming, on God's side, just read the 18th and 19th chapters of Revelation in the Bible. It reads like it is speaking to us in our day, about what the world's rich and powerful are doing in their alliance with "Babylon the Great." (18:2) It speaks of a great alliance, coming to its final, ultimate end. It speaks of the wrath of the Son of God on just such an alliance.

Fallen! Fallen is Babylon the Great!

She has become a home for demons

and a haunt for every evil spirit,

a haunt for every unclean and detestable bird.

For all the nations had drunk

the maddening wine of her adulteries.

The kings of the earth committed adultery with her,

and the merchants of the earth grew rich from her excessive luxuries.
(Rev.18:2-3)

I am no prophet, and neither is there anyone who should consider themselves one. Jesus was the final prophet in the sense of an Old Testament prophet who knows and predicts the future, and he said no one would know what these final events of end times might be (Matthew 24:36-51 & Zachariah 13:1-6). So, what I am about to say is merely a consideration for my readers.

I suggest that the alliance the Bible speaks of, between the Beast and the false Prophet (Rev.19:10), is one between Rome and Islam, who together will attempt to rule the world (see the immigration "problem" in Europe). Consider the Roman Catholic prophesy by St. Malachy, that there will be 262 Popes and then the end will come and the City on Seven Hills will be destroyed. This Pope, Francis, is #262, and will be the last one according to Malachy. Now, I lend no weight to this man's musings. But, within Roman Catholic circles, what Malachy said is being combined with the great amount of distrust and disgust Roman Catholics have with the Pontiff at this time that it is causing a growing crisis.

Significantly, Francis is the first Jesuit pope, finally combining what is called the Black Pope (leader of the Jesuits) and the official Pope into one office. According to many Roman Catholic lay-person-run resources and websites, the mood for yet another pope is greatly diminishing. There is anger at what they perceive as a betrayal of the Vatican to what they always thought was a Christian body, and large numbers who still attend the Mass talk of parting with her. We could expect the next person to sit on the throne of the Vatican to be the ultimate Antichrist, in an effort to bring dissident Roman Catholics back under her fold, and to punish the world for not submitting to the Supreme Pontiff.

What the world's elite, in league with the Vatican, are planning has the possibility of fulfilling so many biblical prophesies, not just for a handful of nations, but for the whole world. For the first time in history not only the plan to form a world-wide totalitarian government is in place, backed and organized by every international organization that we are aware of, but the motivation is there too. We live in the most peaceful and prosperous time in history. There are scientific breakthroughs which are about to happen which would dramatically increase the prosperity and health of the average person in the world. Access to this information is available to people all over the world. Many people know and are suspicious of that handful of people who want to run the world in a totalitarian way. The window for those who want to run the world is closing by the day, and they know it. With the internet, it is now possible for even a one world currency, like that spoken of in Revelation 13:17.

Whatever is coming, it seems to be clear that a great conflict is inevitable. Perhaps the greatest the world has ever seen—even greater than WW2 is coming. The Bible predicts it. I suggest that we should be looking at the skies, looking for the Second Coming of Christ Jesus.

After this I heard what sounded like the roar of a great multitude in heaven shouting:

"Hallelujah!

Salvation and glory and power belong to our God,

for true and just are his judgements.

He has condemned the great prostitute

who corrupted the earth by her adulteries.